Montessori Toddler Discipline

The Ultimate Guide to Parenting Your Children Using Positive Discipline the Montessori Way, Including Examples of Activities that Foster Creative Thinking

© Copyright 2020

This document is geared towards providing exact and reliable information regarding the topic and issue covered. The publication is sold with the idea that the publisher is not required to render accounting, officially permitted, or otherwise, qualified services. If advice is necessary, legal or professional, a practiced individual in the profession should be ordered.

From a Declaration of Principles accepted and approved equally by a Committee of the American Bar Association and a Committee of Publishers and Associations.

In no way is it legal to reproduce, duplicate, or transmit any part of this document in either electronic means or in printed format. Recording of this publication is strictly prohibited and any storage of this document is not allowed unless with written permission from the publisher. All rights reserved.

The information provided is stated to be truthful and consistent, in that any liability, in terms of inattention or otherwise, by any usage or abuse of any policies, processes, or directions contained within is the solitary and utter responsibility of the recipient reader. Under no circumstances will any legal responsibility or blame be held against the publisher for any reparation, damages, or monetary loss due to the information herein, either directly or indirectly.

Respective authors own all copyrights not held by the publisher.

The information herein is offered for informational purposes solely, and is universal as so. The presentation of the information is without contract or any guarantee assurance.

The trademarks used are without any consent, and the publication of the trademark is without permission or backing by the trademark owner. All trademarks and brands within this book are for clarifying purposes only and are the owned by the owners themselves, not affiliated with this document.

Contents

INTRODUCTION 1
CHAPTER 1: THE HISTORY OF MONTESSORI EDUCATION 2
    HOW MARIA MONTESSORI CHANGED EDUCATION 3
    BRIEF HISTORY OF THE MONTESSORI METHOD OF EDUCATION 3
    THREE COMPONENTS OF THE MONTESSORI EDUCATION METHOD 6
    REAL-LIFE STORIES OF THE MONTESSORI SYSTEM AND COMPONENTS 8
CHAPTER 2: MONTESSORI PRINCIPLES AND ACTIVITIES 10
    PRINCIPLE: "TEACHER WAYS AND CHILD WAYS" OR THE RESPECT
    PRINCIPLE 11
    PRINCIPLE: ORDER IN ENVIRONMENT AND MIND 14
    REMAINING PRINCIPLES 17
CHAPTER 3: CHANGING YOUR PERCEPTION 20
    QUICK INSIGHT INTO BRAIN DEVELOPMENT FROM 1 TO 3 YEARS OF AGE 21
    UNDERSTANDING A CHILD'S PERSPECTIVE ON LIFE 22
    A FEW SPECIFIC THINGS THAT IMPACT YOUR CHILD DIRECTLY 22
CHAPTER 4: OBSERVING YOUR CHILD 29
    THE INSTRUCTION MANUAL EVERY PARENT DREAMS OF 29
    UNDERSTANDING SCHEMAS AND SENSITIVE MOODS 31
    EIGHT STAGES OF OBSERVATION 32

CHAPTER 5: SETTING UP YOUR MONTESSORI HOME 37
ROOM BY ROOM MONTESSORI STYLE 39
CHAPTER 6: COORDINATION AND SENSORY ACTIVITIES 44
COORDINATION AND SENSORY IN MONTESSORI 44
CHAPTER 7: HELPING AROUND THE HOUSE 55
WHAT CAN YOUR CHILD ACTUALLY DO? 56
HOW ARE "CHORES" A PART OF YOUR CHILD'S MONTESSORI EXPERIENCE? 59
SHOW, SHOW, SHOW, THEN OBSERVE, AND ALWAYS INVOLVE 60
CHAPTER 8: MUSIC, MOVEMENT, AND MONTESSORI 62
WHAT CHILDREN LEARN FROM MUSIC AND MOVEMENT 63
WHEN DID MUSIC BECOME PART OF THE MONTESSORI MODEL? 64
HOW TO BRING MUSIC INTO YOUR HOME 65
GET TODDLERS MOVING AND GROOVING WITH THESE MONTESSORI MUSIC AND DANCE ACTIVITIES 67
MUSICIANS FROM MONTESSORI TEACHING 69
CHAPTER 9: LEARNING NEW SKILLS THE MONTESSORI WAY 71
CHALLENGES MONTESSORI PARENTS AND TEACHERS HAVE ADJUSTING TO NEW SKILL DEVELOPMENT METHODS 72
LANGUAGE AND SPEECH SKILLS 72
NUMBER SKILLS AND CONCEPT DEVELOPMENT 74
DEVELOPING WRITING SKILLS 75
CHAPTER 10: INTERESTING ARTS AND CRAFTS FOR CREATIVE TODDLER 78
ARTS AND CRAFTS BUILD IMAGINATION AND MORE 79
CHAPTER 11: POSITIVE DISCIPLINE IN THE MONTESSORI HOME 85
BE PROACTIVE - THE FOUNDATION FOR POSITIVE DISCIPLINE 86
WHAT IS SELF-DISCIPLINE? 88
ELEMENTS OF POSITIVE DISCIPLINE 89
WHAT HAPPENS WHEN CHILDREN BREAK THE RULES? 90
BITING, SCRATCHING, HAIR PULLING, AND OTHER PHYSICAL ATTACKS 91
REGARDING SHARING 92

SPECIAL NOTE FOR THE PARENTS 93
CHAPTER 12: GROWING MONTESSORI 94
    KEY TIMES IN PHYSICAL DEVELOPMENT HAPPEN IN THE EARLY YEARS 95
    GROWING UP CHALLENGES 96
    TOYS THAT GROW WITH THEM 97
    PARENTING HABITS CHANGE AND ADAPT 99
CONCLUSION 102
HERE'S ANOTHER BOOK BY MERYL KAUFMAN THAT YOU MIGHT LIKE 103
REFERENCES 104

Introduction

Maria Montessori forever changed education when she acknowledged that children, particularly young children, might do best with less adult interference. She pushed against the norms of the time, suggesting positive discipline, fostering creativity, and encouraging independence from a very young age. Now, you can take her teachings and bring them into your home. You need not enroll your toddler in a Montessori school to get a head start with your child. Learn what it means to observe, build independence, and support your child through positive discipline methods.

Throughout this book, we'll explore what parents report as successful, and others report as not so thrilling. There are a variety of activities in nearly every chapter and a thorough explanation of the rich history and thoughtful development of each aspect of the Montessori environment.

Learn what it takes to get started and to grow Montessori skills with your child. Have all of your questions regarding using the Montessori Method with toddlers answered right here. You'll discover activities you can do today and identify opportunities to help your child engage and grow into a wonderful person.

Chapter 1: The History of Montessori Education

For most parents of toddlers, Montessori seems like an out of reach abstract concept that many teachers have very strong opinions about. Maria Montessori changed education dramatically, and when she developed this particular form of education, it raised a lot of questions. The Montessori method challenges a lot of traditional systems and techniques, even the methods used in schools today.

So, what is the difference between Montessori education and standard or traditional education? Italian physician Maria Montessori developed Montessori education. It is a child-centric approach to education that uses the foundation of the scientific method. It calls upon observation, hypotheses, experimentation, and conclusions. The Montessori method has been around for over 100 years.

With anything this revolutionary, there are a lot of questions, concerns, and misconceptions. Throughout this book, you'll have the opportunity to grasp the three components of Montessori teaching, Montessori discipline, the foundation of the Montessori method, and more. We dive deep into different elements that commonly appear in early childhood Montessori classrooms, and ways that parents have adopted the Montessori method for their home.

Here is a short history and easy introduction into Montessori and what to expect by bringing Montessori teachings into your home.

How Maria Montessori Changed Education

Born on August 31, 1870, Maria Montessori broke down educational barriers early in life. At 13, she entered an all-boys school and quickly excelled in science and mathematics. Much of Montessori's childhood has become legend. Maria Montessori is widely known and acknowledged as the first woman to graduate from medical school in Italy. However, Italy's first female physician was actually Dorotea Bucca. Montessori followed shortly after and was unfazed not to become the first female physician as she quickly identified that the position wasn't for her.

In 1896, she changed the course of her career by returning to the University of Rome to learn about psychology and philosophy and apply that knowledge to teaching children. Then, working as a child psychiatrist, she developed her craft and her understanding of childhood development.

Throughout her lifetime, Maria Montessori worked as a professor of anthropology at the University of Rome. She opened her own school in Rome, schools around the world, and drastically changed how educators and psychiatrists treated and worked with children. It was an eventful life, and she was nominated for the Nobel Peace Prize three years in a row proceeding her death. These nominations happened in 1949, 1950, and 1951. Maria Montessori died in Holland in 1952.

Brief History of the Montessori Method of Education

We briefly covered Maria Montessori's history as a person, but the Montessori method of education has a much more intricate timeline. In the years leading to 1906, Maria Montessori used her experience and education as a physician, psychologist, and philosopher to research and work directly with children with disabilities. She quickly identified that the needs of children with disabilities and the needs of children were much the same. They were also much unacknowledged in traditional childhood education. So, in 1906, Dr. Montessori opened Casa Dei Bambini or "Children's House."

The purpose of the Children's House was to provide education among 60 underprivileged children; all were Italian, all were underprivileged, and all showed an amazing response to the materials provided in the Children's House. Doctor Montessori used methods of scientific observation and identified that children were not only capable of deep concentration but often entered into states of peace and calm rather than outbursts and tantrums. After a few years of observation, Montessori acknowledged publicly that when given the proper environment, you can discover and provoke a child's true nature. Doctor Montessori used the term *normalization* to describe this change.

During the Children's House's early years, Montessori simply observed. She sat still and watched how the children played and interacted together. As she observed, she saw where different children excelled, and some struggled. With age-groupings larger than you would find in a traditional class, the older students tended to the younger. Children were more apt to turn toward an older peer than seek an adult or teacher. She acknowledged that through the process of that normalization, children were more apt to coordinate and cooperate with each other.

After many years of working in Rome, Montessori made her way to the United States. In 1913, Montessori, working alongside Alexander Graham Bell and his wife, founded America's first Montessori Association. The Montessori Educational Association is still the primarily recognized Montessori Authority in America. Montessori did not stay in the United States, but did visit again in 1915 as part of the Panama Pacific International Exhibition. At this exhibition in

1915, she unveiled The Glass House classroom exhibit. She was furthering the idea that observation and not being acknowledged or seen by the children was the best way to see children thrive in their natural habitat.

Montessori kept pushing for change within education systems and awareness across the globe. She was shining a spotlight, not only on all the things that were widely done wrong, but also on all the ways that communities and educators could change education in a positive way for the children.

In 1917, Spain invited Maria Montessori to open a research institute. The government requested that she spend time establishing an institute where children could learn the Montessori method. Montessori obliged and opened the Spanish Research Institute that year. In 1919, Montessori made her way to England. In London, she hosted a series of teacher courses in London where educators could receive training on child psychiatry and the Montessori method. The United Kingdom appointed Montessori as a government inspector of schools in 1922. In 1929, Montessori saw a new level of success as she opened the Association Montessori International, or AMI.

During her travels and between her major successful milestones, Montessori was well known for returning to her home in Italy. Unfortunately, Maria Montessori was driven out of Italy in 1934 for opposing Mussolini. Some also say that she spent the remainder of her life traveling across Europe and occasionally visiting the United States. However, she could never return to Italy.

In 1938, the first Montessori Training Center opened in the Netherlands, and in 1939 India began a series of training courses. Montessori's last major milestone in expanding her education Empire was 1949 when London finally opened its first Montessori Center. Although Montessori was welcomed in the United Kingdom and had served in different positions within the education community, she hadn't been able to get a Montessori Center off the ground. This final achievement, founding the Montessori Center in London, shortly preceded her first nomination for the Nobel Peace Prize.

Following the death of Maria Montessori, there was a lot of scrutiny and changes to the name "Montessori." Mario Montessori, her son (and often collaborator), handled the foundations differently than Maria Montessori. Ultimately, absent copyrights or other protection, almost every country could open Montessori schools, and anyone could use the term "Montessori."

As of 2020, there were over 20,000 Montessori schools internationally, with the United States playing host to 5,000. However, only 1,100 are recognized by the Montessori Educational Association.

Three Components of the Montessori Education Method

There are three vital elements of the Montessori education method. As we mentioned, almost anyone can use the name *Montessori*, but if you notice that any of the three Montessori elements are missing, then it's not true Montessori education. These elements are the adult, often called the directress or teacher, the environment, and the apparatus.

The adult in your situation, most likely the parent, has to prepare themselves before they work directly with the children. The adult needs to understand what passive guidance means. Adults should not be forceful or authoritative, which is a huge challenge for parents. Parents often face scrutiny no matter what they do. If they don't step in during a baby fight or when children have problems, then someone always has something to say. If they do step in, someone also has something to say. There is no "right" way to appease everyone, and with the Montessori Method, teachers and parents choose the less forceful or authoritative approach. So, you'll model the behavior you want them to learn, such as good manners and peaceful interaction.

Adults in the Montessori circle are more of a guide or mentor rather than a dictator.

Special note on changing roles: homeschooling or using Montessori at home means that you're more than a parent or caregiver, but think back to past times when this was the norm. Our separation between parenting and teaching is recent, and something you can overcome. You can love, nurture, and create a substantial learning environment. You can also discipline and help your child understand what is and what is not acceptable. It's tough at first, but after the first six months to a year, it gets much easier.

The Montessori environment is a prepared space that encourages exploration and engagement. This environment invites toddlers and young children to touch, make noise, move items, and to live actively within their environment. Ideally, in the Montessori environment, any child can perform any of their daily activities independently or with minimal assistance. For example, they should have access to their clothing, toys, bed, and other areas of their living space. In another chapter, we cover exactly how to build a positive Montessori environment right in your home. It is not a replica of what you would find in a Montessori classroom, but it can help promote independence and exploration with your toddler. And the Montessori environment should, above all else, focus on safety. Through using size-appropriate furniture and removing common dangers, your child can feel safe in the household. You'll also find some relief in not trying to rush in every other moment because something is teetering, or something feels unsafe.

Initially called the Montessori apparatus, this element refers specifically to Montessori approved tools and materials. Because of limited protection on the title Montessori, you might find many toys and furnishings that claim to fall in line with Montessori practices but aren't part of the Montessori apparatus. The Montessori apparatus refers specifically to sensorial materials, namely popular toys such as the Pink Tower, the sorting bears, sound tubes, and some other tools.

Maria Montessori refers to these toys as tools and materials rather than playthings. You'll notice that most of these toys are wooden, and most of them are open play or designed for limitless play. They may have an intended purpose, such as The Pink Tower, which was meant for stacking. However, there's nothing wrong with playing with it in many other ways. In different chapters of this book will talk about tools that are specific to that activity or section of development.

Real-Life Stories of the Montessori System and Components

Montessori schools across the world have produced world-renowned artists, businesspeople, musicians, engineers, and leaders in the tech industry. Many of these successful people credit their time spent in Montessori education and emphasize the importance of creativity and exploration. Each of these people has given a fair amount of attention to the time they spent under Montessori style education, and some have directly credited it with the early development of their interests.

Famous Montessori Success Stories

Will Wright created The Sims, a highly successful game franchise through the Maxis and Electronic Arts labels. Wright performed a TEDx Talk that directly addressed how the Montessori education he had as a young child inspired him to build open-ended games. The Sims was among the first of its kind as a "sandbox" game without an end-goal and instead focuses on life lessons. Wright does acknowledge that architecture and architectural design always interested him, and it lent itself to The Sims design. The TEDx Talk talked about the gaming communities, an overwhelming amount of shooters, and guided-story games. While true, Wright didn't speak out against his fellow developers and engineers. Instead, he simply continued developing The Sims.

Jeff Bezos stands among a small circle of businesspeople who've led a company to such heights of success. However, he's among an even smaller circle of people who've taken a company from three years of extreme debt into the success that Amazon is today. Jeff Bezos, CEO and creator of Amazon not only attended and clearly benefited from Montessori education but is a very public proponent. In 2018, Bezos announced that he would use $2 billion to help aid struggling families and develop an accessible preschool network. By September 2018, he had made good on the first half of his promise by investing $1 billion into opening new Montessori-inspired schools in areas that needed it most.

Other Montessori success stories include both Google founders, Sergei Brin and Larry Page. In fact, there are an extraordinary number of Montessori-educated people in high positions within the tech industry. So much so that news media outlets have taken to calling them the "Montessori Mafia," and it's clear that it has some weight as many are pouring investments into promoting or opening Montessori-inspired preschools across the nation.

These success stories offer only a touch of insight into what someone can accomplish with the right environment and development early in life. Maria Montessori saw children for what they are: opportunity. Each little person is a ball of opportunity if only we can focus on their interests, curiosity, and developing new and exciting ways to engage that child. With your support, not only as a parent but as a humble leader in the Montessori Method, your child can have that nurturing engagement while learning about the world around them.

Chapter 2: Montessori Principles and Activities

Montessori relies on a handful of fundamental principles which lay out the expectation for different activities. These activities tie into different principles that can help the child and the parent or teacher. Through understanding the application of these tenets, teachers and parents can exercise their understanding together. So, what are the principles?

The Montessori Principles are overarching guides, and, as with most other Montessori elements, they offer as much guidance as confusion. Where many people lose track of the core of Montessori is in the principles. As with many guiding texts, these doctrines can have different interpretations, and some people take them to extremes greater than others. It's always best to keep in mind that Montessori herself meant for these to serve at face value – a what-you-see-is-what-you-get mentality is often best when working with this philosophy. There is no need to overcomplicate, overthink, or overact. Imagine these principles exist only in their most simple state.

The activities work to support that idea. The concept that simplest is best resounds throughout Montessori activities and educational approaches. For each principle, we have explained it in the most transparent way, but also provided a correlating activity and an adaptive explanation for application with toddlers. Toddler discipline can set the stage for early childhood development. By starting the Montessori method earlier in life, these principles can be well-honed and in full use by the time they reach kindergarten age.

Principle: "Teacher Ways and Child Ways" or The Respect Principle

One of the eight principles of the Montessori method is there are teacher ways and child ways. Often this boils down to adult interaction and how much interaction is appropriate. Montessori teachers, or *true Montessori teachers*, should have extensive training and years of practice on how to guide and promote independence while still remaining a teacher.

Put simply, there are ways you do things, and there are ways that children or toddlers do things, and they are different. It is not a my-way-or-the-highway situation and it is also not the difference between right and wrong. It is simply this tiny human perceives the world without the decades of knowledge that you've accumulated. They also see the world from a physically different angle. What seems appropriate or reasonable to a toddler or child may seem outlandish and frustrating to an adult because you not only have a deeper understanding of the way the world works but have an easier time accessing the world.

The point of this principle is that adults should allow children to struggle so they can learn. There is a point where adults should step in before frustration takes over. With toddlers, this is frustrating for the adult involved because they may not know when to ask for help or may be so immersed in building independence they refuse help or don't want it.

It is possible to offer too much guidance, and it is possible to be too absent. This principle is a constant work in progress. Even the most skilled Montessori educators have to return to this principle constantly as their guiding light.

If there is one takeaway from this principle, it is to view your interaction and guidance through the lesson of Goldilocks and the Three Bears. When evaluating your interactions with your child, ask is it too much? Is it too little? Or is it just right? Of course, you must change your perception of what you think is *just right* to what is just right for your toddler.

Example

A great example of this is a toddler learning to dress. A lot of toddlers have strong opinions about their clothes and want independence when getting dressed. Some toddlers would rather be naked all the time. They might hate clothes or feel that clothes are confining or know that putting on clothes means leaving the house and they don't want to do that.

Other toddlers love getting dressed. They might love it so much they demand multiple wardrobe changes throughout the day. They might insist on picking out what they wear, and shake their head no at every offer from their closet or dresser until they reach the last item available.

As an example, we will use Emily. Little Emily loves getting dressed. She loves picking out her own dresses and finding different accessories such as tights, headbands, and bows. Emily loves changing her clothes throughout the day, and sometimes throws a fit or a tantrum that results in three or four wardrobe changes. It is frustrating for her parents, and it's frustrating for Emily.

How can you approach this particularly sore subject through the Montessori principle of child ways and adult ways?

First, to align the environment, the parents involved should give Emily access to her clothes and accessories. It can lead to more mess, but it can also promote independence, and she might choose what she wants to wear the first time she gets dressed instead of changing clothes so often.

Second, unlike outfits that involve full pants, dresses are easy to manage even with small hands. When Emily wants to get dressed in the morning, her parents may hand her the dress she wants and ask her to do it herself. Emily will struggle at first and may need guidance with getting her head into the right hole or sliding her arms up, but this is a skill toddlers can learn quickly.

Third, continue consistency with asking that Emily dress herself, and watch as she tries different ways. If true frustration takes over to where Emily would rather not get dressed, then the adult should step in and provide more guidance.

Now, Emily may not get dressed how her parents dress her. She may put her arms in first and then push the dress over her head. She may put her head in first and then flip her arms into place. Emily might step into the dress from the top down and shimmy it up until it's right.

Returning to this key principle, Emily is doing what makes sense and is most accessible for her. She can find her processes as she grows and spends more time dressing. There are child ways, and there are adult ways; neither is inherently incorrect.

Activity

We are just getting dressed as an example, but let's look at stacking activities. Take blocks of different sizes and shapes, and put them in front of your toddler.

Most adults know that to create some sort of stable structure, you would use the biggest blocks at the bottom, the medium blocks in the middle, and the smallest blocks at the top.

We promise that, at least on the first run, your toddler will not follow that recipe for a sturdy structure. They may not even create a structure. They may create a line of blocks and are not inclined to build upward. A toddler might put the smallest blocks on the bottom, and then put the bigger blocks on top. They may even use the smaller blocks and create a single tower that goes straight up.

Use this activity as an observation opportunity. Later, we'll dive deeper into observation and how to do it properly. This activity is also a great way to exercise your patience and deal with frustrations when your child isn't doing something the way you expect them to do or how you know produces a better result. Let your child play with the blocks and know that they are exercising their way of doing things as they go through this activity.

You might offer more guidance, such as suggesting that you build a castle or make a tower of blocks that goes straight up. This guidance can help you see the different ways they approach these projects.

Principle: Order in Environment and Mind

The environment is a huge factor in the Montessori method and education. However, the person who possibly said it best is neither a Montessori advocate nor an age-old teacher. Ruben, a rising star in personal development and exploring happiness, offered the phrase, "Outer order, inner calm."

Outer order inner calm is as true for toddlers as it is for adults. When the environment is consistent, static, predictable, and in order, it takes mental stress off of any situation that happens in that environment. Your toddler's environment should be both calm and orderly. Toddlers enjoy spacious areas where they can move around, but there's also an underwhelming factor. If you have gone into a Montessori classroom, you might have noticed the minimalistic approach to displaying toys and activities.

Fortunately, this principle is one that you will have to return to again and again. In a later chapter, we explain what you should expect and establish for your child in a Montessori-friendly environment. Once these changes are put into place, you simply have to maintain them. You may occasionally have the urge to change things up or move things around, but once the order is established, you have to pick only up and return things to their place.

Now, most parents struggle to keep general living areas tidy, and following the tornado of mess a toddler leaves behind may make neatness seem like the impossible dream. In our example and the activity provided for this principle, we will dive into exactly how this principle applies to you and your toddler. You are not a one-person maid service picking up after every mess your toddler creates.

This principle builds the foundation for a respectful relationship between adult and child. Remember, keep order in the environment and in mind.

Example

You need not look too far to find an example of how a toddler can set an environment into disorder. Many parents struggle with this particular principle because it seems as though it sets them and their children on opposite sides. We promise it is not you versus your child.

Let's look at an example that should seem very familiar to any parent. A toddler's play area is becoming a disaster; it doesn't . matter if their play area is primarily in a living room, a nursery, playroom, or the toddler's bedroom. Deshawna loves playing pretend, and she will drag out every stuffed animal and doll to create elaborate parties. These parties might involve dress-up, fake food, real food, tea sets, movie screenings, and even just general mayhem. At the end of the day, there are countless stuffed animals and dolls scattered throughout the room. Plus, all of the toys or day-to-day objects that got dragged out to be part of the pretend play too.

If your response to Deshawna is frustrated outbursts, you wouldn't be the first parent to lose their temper over such a mess. If your response to Deshawna is to pick it up yourself so you didn't have to deal with the argument, you wouldn't be the first parent to choose the passive approach. When parents face a level-10 mess, they may experience frustration, anger, fall into a weepy puddle on the floor, or completely give up and just let the mess exist until they can mentally deal with it.

A mess from playtime is not the only thing that parents have to concern themselves with, and often this disorder in the environment leads us to disorder in mind. It's no wonder that when confronted with this much and disorder in our physical space that we act irrationally.

Activity

Wait, there are activities to help?

Don't get too excited; this is more of a Mary Poppins (minus the magic) approach. There are Montessori tools that engage children in the cleaning process and teach them life skills for cleaning up after themselves.

Mary Poppins is the one that claimed that every job is a game, but the iconic line of, "Well begun is half done," comes directly from Aristotle. You can take both elements and implement them into your daily cleaning. Involve your toddler in cleaning through every step. You are not only introducing them to the idea that we all have to pick up after ourselves, but you're showing them what you do that contributes to a clean environment. Your toddler may not be on board at first. This is one time where Montessori parents do tend to blend authoritative and modeling approaches.

You need not force your child to clean. But you might put your foot down when it comes to breaking out another toy or starting a new mess before the environment is ready. You can tell your child that until the blocks are put away, the room isn't ready to play in. The phrasing you use in cleaning activities is important. When you're cleaning an area and trying to get your toddler involved, or at least having them patiently observe you while you clean, try these phrases:

- "We can play with _____ faster if you helped clean up."
- "We clean so that we have all this space back."

- "After every mess, we have to clean up."
- "I feel so much better when we're done cleaning, but I don't feel good when our room isn't clean."

For some parents, that language can sound a little pandering, but using "we" and "our" instead of me and you is important. The small changes in a language like this can even follow you into adult conversations. Most fights and arguments revolve around you-centric language. Using shared language offers a degree of mutual respect.

You're acknowledging that this is your space, but it is also a space for your toddler. It is where they live and where they should contribute to cleanliness.

Montessori tools that address this principle are really scaled-down versions of adult cleaning tools. Toddler size brooms are relatively easy to find, and you can swap out dish towels for washcloths, or rip a paper towel in half.

When the right tools are available, most adults find they need not clean on their own for long. When you emphasize the benefits of a clean area, toddlers pick up on the behavior you model. When you model cleanliness, especially with a decent attitude, they will likely jump in to help do the job faster.

Remaining Principles

The remaining principles are largely attributed to the first two big concepts we covered but focus on specific elements of learning and development. Once you have the first two big principles in place, the other principles will come much easier and can offer even more benefits for the child and the parent-child relationship.

Principle: Movement and Cognition

Movement and cognition are most recognizable as normalization. In chapter one, we reference normalization as Montessori's term for children behaving in their natural state. The principle is that movement and cognition should happen in tandem and that by presenting activities that engage both movement and cognition, the child learns better.

The most common example of this is independent playtime. When children are permitted to play independently with whatever toy catches their eye, you can watch them engage in different movement behaviors and see they are thinking through the scientific process. Although it may seem like they're only stacking blocks or spreading beads, they're also thinking... *Why does this work this way? What if I do this differently? How does this work?*

A great activity to promote movement and cognition is bead threading. Another great activity for movement and cognition is sorting. Provide your child with a few different items to sort by color or type and watch how they carefully pick them apart and sort them into different groups.

Principle: Choice

Choice is a massive principal in Montessori teaching, and it addresses both respect for the child and sensitive periods. In an earlier example, we noted the choice of getting dressed and wearing what the child wanted. This is an outstanding example of this principle, as children often feel differently about activities or daily routines when they have a choice in the matter.

You can implement choice into almost any part of your day. But, to get started, make an activity choosing between two items. You can use this again and again throughout the day. Start your day by asking if the child wants to wear the red shirt or the blue shirt. Then when it's bath time, ask if they would like the white towel or the brown towel. You can even bring this into eating. Does your child prefer apples or grapes? Maybe they would rather sit in their highchair than at their tiny table. With the activity of presenting toys, start with only two choices. Toddlers are learning a lot, and they're easily overwhelmed with choices. By presenting four or five different shirts or having *anything* in the refrigerator as an option, they may experience choice paralysis.

Principle: Absorbent Mind

The absorbent mind largely relies on children learning through experience, and by learning through experience, they develop agency, independence, and confidence. This largely plays into the first principle. However, it takes a different angle about independence and learning.

Instead of acknowledging the adult way and the child way, this is more about adult restriction. Restrain the urge to say *no* or to speed up a process because something is taking too long. The activity here is more for the adult. Try carrying around a small notebook or even use a tally counter on your phone. Then, mark a tally each time you felt the need to interject into what your child was doing. You can go the extra mile and make notes about why the interjection wasn't necessary, but you'll get the message loud and clear at the end of the day when you have a page full of tally marks.

Chapter 3: Changing Your Perception

Before we can dive directly into implementing Montessori methods and activities, we need to re-evaluate our perception. Teenagers often complain that adults have forgotten what it was like to be a teenager, but toddlers don't even have the communication skills or insight to explain that. We don't know what it was like to live like a toddler; most of us have forgotten. And most of us have little empathy for how children and toddlers view their world and how our perception towards education and learning impact them.

The Montessori method largely dispels the notion of punishment, restriction of freedom, and traditional roles of a caretaker. Many parents wish they could put the idea of punishment aside; Montessori also calls for a drastic decrease in encouragement. It's a challenge, no matter which way you look at it. It is a challenge to change your lens on how you view your child and the expectations you set. However, the payoff can be massive. By not praising, and by avoiding discipline, you're able to watch and appreciate your child's natural curiosity and development. This may be one of the more difficult chapters, and you might need to return to it again and again because changing our perception as parents and adults does not come easily.

Quick Insight Into Brain Development from 1 to 3 Years of Age

Most parents have experienced a long path during pregnancy and infancy and know that, to some degree, what they do affects their child. Childhood development is so malleable, and as parents we know that but, still, we are only human. So, what do toddlers experience between the ages of one and three regarding brain development?

Brain development is possibly at its peak during the toddler years. Toddlers understand and remember shapes, size, color, routine, numbers, songs, animals, and more. They are taking all the sensory exploration from infancy and actually putting it into practice. Positive and negative experiences will directly affect brain development. These experiences will affect them as much as proper nutrition. By the time a child reaches age six, their brain has gained about four pounds in weight and developed between 75 and 90 percent of its complete adult brain weight. Their brains develop about 700 new neuron connections per minute. That is incredible!

However, so much of the toddler's brain is still developing. The prefrontal cortex is not developed enough for anyone at that age to make reasonable or logic-based decisions. Additionally, the limbic system is still running the show. The limbic system is the part of the brain that operates at its most basic state. Hunger, sleep, and more are what come from the limbic system, and because of their irrational processing center, it is easy for the toddler to quickly "lose it," especially over food, sleep, or wanting to do something "their" way.

Toddlers are in stage two of brain development where they're working on reasoning, perception, attachment, emotional understanding, working memory, and life experiences.

Understanding a Child's Perspective on Life

Literally, their entire perspective is different. While you're standing in line at the grocery store, you see the back of the head of the person in front of you. Your child sees that person's pockets, maybe the bottom of the conveyer, and that enticing rack of candy.

Children are usually between three and four feet shorter than standard adults, with smaller hands, smaller steps, and largely, we expect them to just live in our world. As adults, we get irritated when they take too long to tackle a simple task. We walk at a typical pace and aren't inherently astounded these tiny humans can keep up quite often. There's also the frustration that they're so interested in what we're doing that they interject themselves into our activity and simply can't have the same experience. They can't use knives, climb ladders, jump into the deep end without protection, and more. But, as adults, and as people, we're prone to not having easy access to different perspectives. We need to take occasional, purposeful action to dive into the child's perspective. A lot of this you can accomplish by playing with your child and observing them.

They not only see things differently, but they think about things differently. They don't have the knowledge you have, or the height you have, or the tactile abilities for intricate finger movements you have. So, when we can see the world through a child's lens, take that moment and watch them or play.

A Few Specific Things That Impact Your Child Directly

There are things that we heard and experienced as children we are now using in our parental practice. Maria Montessori had a revolutionary impact because of how she broke away from traditional methods of interacting with children of all ages. Here are a few things that often come from the parenting perspective not entirely considerate of the child's perspective. Some of these seem innate, things we do naturally, and feel natural as an adult. Others are something we may have let slip. Either way, here are a few of the most common situations that can affect the child's perception of the world around them, and changing these behaviors could help you understand the child's perception of life.

"Good Girl/Boy/They/Person"

Telling a child they are good is not inherently a bad thing. However, using the phrase sparingly or only when they seem to do what you want, could be causing harm. If you ask them to take a seat to eat their meal and acknowledge that they're a good girl or a good boy, it ties obedience to good behavior. For many parents, that's perfectly acceptable, and most parents strive to have their children listen to them. Having a child listen to you as a parent can be a matter of safety. If your child darts towards the street and you say *stop*, and they stopped, it could have saved their life. However, the question comes up of how obedient do you want your child to be with other adults? Do you want an adult you don't know telling your kid they are a good girl or a good boy and going through behavior that is inappropriate or unacceptable or maybe just not in line with your parenting? Probably not.

There is another problem with the good girl and good boy terms. Going beyond obedience and listening blindly, there's the matter of the unsaid factor of this phrase. If they are good, sometimes it means they are also bad.

If you say "good girl" when your child is listening, then it means that they're not good when they're not listening. However, a child exploring something or having a curiosity that doesn't fit in line with social norms isn't behaving badly. They're doing what their brain is supposed to do at that age. Their brain is expanding and developing rapidly during these three to five years, and exploration and curiosity are the driving elements of that development.

"That's Dangerous" - When It's Really Not

Most parents are probably prone to this one, and they may not even realize how it's affecting their child's perception of the world around them. We often say that something is dangerous when maybe it's really not. Touching a hot plate will deliver a burn, but it's not going to deliver a second-degree burn or a third-degree burn. Just the same as when a child picks up a pair of scissors that can become dangerous, but the overall reaction of jumping in and ripping the scissors out of the child's hand can cause more harm than simply asking for them to put the scissors down. If they don't listen and respond appropriately to request such as putting sharp objects down or handing them to you nicely, then change direction and be a little more assertive.

Often, we respond that something is dangerous when maybe it would just cause very mild harm or discomfort, and it's usually because we just don't want them to do what they are doing. We don't want children to touch the oven door, even though the oven door doesn't get that hot. We don't want them to walk on the edge of the sidewalk because we inherently feel that the next step is to leave the sidewalk. We're scolding them now rather than holding them when they do actually do something dangerous. This comes from good intentions. We see the possible dangers ahead, but our children live in the present moment. Toddlers are not worried about the consequences of moving from the edge of the sidewalk to stepping onto the road because all they're worried about is walking on the edge of the sidewalk.

One of the best Montessori methods that comes with handling possibly dangerous activity or something that could potentially cause discomfort is redirection. Redirection allows the adult in the situation to acknowledge the child's behavior and then pull their attention to something else. You're kind of extorting how much toddlers are immersed at the moment. Let's look at the sidewalk example. You're walking to check the mail when your toddler keeps veering for the very edge of the sidewalk, and you're getting a little nervous. You might have acknowledged how fun it is to walk on the edge but then draw their attention to the flowers growing at the edge of your neighbor's property or how exciting it is to get closer and closer to the mailbox. You might let them hold the mail key or ask if they would like to carry the mail on the way back home.

If these don't sound engaging or if they're too forward-thinking for your toddler at this point in time, you might simply redirect their attention to the elements of nature or their immediate surroundings. You can say, "Wow, look at the bird" or even "Hey, the sidewalk is gray, did you see that?"

Tantrums

Tantrums and toddlers go together like peas and carrots, cheese and burgers, potatoes and gravy. You simply can't separate them. Some children are more prone to tantrums and some are more strong-willed or rebellious. But some children rarely have tantrums or are easy going, so tantrums come quickly and subside just as fast.

Covering tantrums also falls under the element of discipline, which we cover in a later chapter. Acknowledging tantrums so far as the child's perception, however, means looking at things from a different angle. Why is your child throwing a tantrum? Because they didn't get their way? Don't you get frustrated when you don't get to your way? Haven't we all seen various viral videos of adults acting like toddlers because they didn't get what they wanted?

Children don't just throw tantrums because they don't get their way. Many toddler tantrums happen because they are communicating basic needs. In their brains, the prefrontal cortex, the decision center, is still under construction. Your child's behavior and wants is largely controlled by their limbic system. That limbic system manages to control basic human needs. Food, water, shelter, and security are the four primary issues of day-to-day life that the limbic system handles. So, if this is the primary ruler of the toddler's brain, then it is more likely that your toddler is throwing a tantrum because one of these four elements isn't met. They could be hungry, thirsty, want to go inside, want to go outside, or feel insecure at that moment.

There are a few different ways to handle tantrums, and some will be covered in the discipline section, but it's worth mentioning it in the *child perception* chapter. The first is to repeat what the child is doing or saying. Some parents have moved towards using the front-facing camera on their phones to show their children what they look like in tantrum mode. By recreating, mimicking, or outright showing your toddler what they look like in the tantrum, even your toddler can understand this communication is not effective. It can take a while, but repeating what they are saying can help draw attention to the communication breakdown.

For example, Don was quietly playing with his cars, and then his world stopped. Don's mom didn't understand what was going on, but she acknowledged that he began throwing his toys across the room and screaming at the top of his lungs. It was a full-fledged tantrum, and the parent has no idea why it started or how to make it stop after a few minutes of handing cars back to the toddler, offering a sippy cup, and attempting to negotiate. The parent loses her cool, points the finger at the toddler, and says, "That is enough. You need to calm down." Does this sound familiar? It is a pretty standard response for an adult who has to handle multiple toddler tantrums per day that can last between 20 seconds and 45 minutes or longer. At some point, we become less empathetic to their perception, especially in highly emotional situations like a tantrum.

What are the tricks of handling a tantrum? The one we mentioned earlier doesn't come from the Montessori method, but instead from <u>The Happiest Toddler on the Block</u>. By repeating exactly what the child is saying, you'll notice that either the child will begin mimicking you, and a classic Daffy Duck and Bugs Bunny "Yes - no - yes - no (turnaround) no - yes" situation. Or your child will begin to use different words, clearly frustrated that you don't understand or that you're not saying what they believe they are saying.

Now, if repeating what your child is saying doesn't work to deescalate the tantrum - because nothing is a foolproof approach with toddlers - you can try ignoring. Rather than telling the child they need to get it together and calm down, you simply acknowledge that you don't feel good either, so you will give them a moment to feel better, and you'll come back when you feel better.

Your Role as a Parent, Caregiver, and Montessori Teacher

Montessori drastically changes what we consider "normal" parenting practices. There are a million and one different ways to raise children, and most are acceptable. But the Montessori approach takes a more nurturing-approach than a direct tactic. You can still be a parent and not just a teacher. You'll likely find that after some adjustment, you may enjoy the time you spend with your child even more by applying the Montessori perception when working as a parent.

Most parents struggle with the adjustment of declining their level of discipline and taking down their level of praise. Praising is discouraged, and there is solid reasoning behind that approach. The issue is that you want the child to explore their interests, not only the interests you praise them for. And the decrease in discipline isn't necessary to let them free-range raise themselves, but to better understand natural consequences and that natural consequences exist in the world.

As a parent, one of the most challenging elements is to balance our roles. We may be a spouse, caregiver, teacher, mother, father, or parent in some other capacity. Then there is the element of personal neglect, where most parents acknowledge that they simply don't have time to decompress or sit down and watch or read something that interests them. To mildly address this, while also brushing up on the Montessori method, we offer this: as a parent, you are already a teacher.

The idea that you and some other unknown person are both necessary to teach your child is not exactly on point. Now, other adults will have many things to instruct your children, and your child will, without a doubt, learn much from their peers. You will probably need to rely on other adults to cover some topics that you may not know or have expertise in. However, you can always teach your child, and simply through doing and existing, your child is constantly learning from you.

Chapter 4: Observing Your Child

Early in life, we spend hours just watching our babies. However, when they get to toddler age, we start distancing ourselves and become less observant. There are terms such as "follow the child," and "freedom" or "leading" that are often misunderstood in Montessori. So, what do these terms mean, and how can you start observing your child? This chapter will cover everything you need to get over the challenges of understanding your child and how to know when to employ these methods.

Just as with most Montessori terms, the ones involved in observation require a bit of teasing out. We will start with the terms, cover the processes, and then dive directly into the directions of how to observe your child with the Montessori lens.

The Instruction Manual Every Parent Dreams Of

How many parents have you heard say something to the effect of, "Gee, I wish kids came with manuals." Without a doubt, many more parents have thought this and not voiced it. Observation is that sought after instruction manual. By closely observing your child at different points in the day, you'll not only notice what sparked their interest but also what they tend to gravitate toward and what they tend to repel.

Observing is difficult for parents. We're biased and prone to thinking our child is just the most fascinating thing, or we're so utterly overwhelmed with all the other demands of parenting that we can't appreciate those moments that we should be observing. Fortunately, you can plan times for observation or conduct your observation when you have a few moments to sit down and simply watch your kid. We don't mean watching in the sense of babysitting and making sure that they don't get into mischief. You'll soon see exactly what we mean by watching and observing.

Let's Sort Out These Confusing Terms

Following the child—The misconception is this means you just trail along to wherever the kid goes. Following the child actually addresses a larger concept. It means establishing a space developmentally appropriate and offers a variety of interests. Often, you don't need to physically shadow the toddler, but instead visually track how they progressed around the room and what captures their interest or attention the most.

Freedom—The use of the word freedom is possibly the most misunderstood term in all the Montessori practices. The idea that Maria Montessori presented was *freedom with limits*. Those limits are put in place environmentally so that often dangerous or questionable activities simply aren't available. Of course, there's always a limit to what children can or should do.

Example: Tim likes to climb. At the playground, and outside, that is fine. However, during an observation period, Tim's dad saw him climb up onto his small play table. Tim's dad was observing but knew that he had to interject because the play table was certainly not sturdy enough to hold the three-year-old's weight for a long. Tim's dad stepped in and offered that they could take their playtime outside where Tim could climb. Timmy's freedom wasn't compromised; his safety was protected. By moving the playtime outside where Tim could climb, he was continuing to exercise his freedom and to build his motor skills in an appropriate environment. That is freedom with limits.

Leading—There are dos and don'ts with leading with Montessori. Ideally, the child will do as much leading as possible. When the adult leads, much of the independence and experimentation are lost. During observation times leading should be at an minimum, and intervention should only happen when the child's safety is at risk, or they are clearly breaking pre-defined rules. Rules such as "only using nice touching" and similar aren't negotiable just because the child is leading.

Understanding Schemas and Sensitive Moods

These are the moments when your child is immovably interested or invested in what they're doing. Schemas, or sensitive moods, can happen at any point, including when they're not necessarily playing with their toys. A toddler may become incessantly involved with their fingernails, or very invested in the prongs of one of their forks.

Now, these moods come in the ways that a creative muse might. They're not predictable, and they are usually not on any type of schedule. So, you may not always capture a toddler or young child in the moment of a schema or sensitive mood during your observation. That is fine, but do take note that if you see your child in a sensitive mood, it may be the time to start an observation.

What you're looking for to determine if your child is in the midst of a schema is the intense focus. Often toddlers cannot innately focus on one thing for long periods. So, if you see that happening, it is not a common instance, and it's a great opportunity to discover what is engaging your child and question why it's holding their attention so well.

Eight Stages of Observation

If you're not observing, then you don't have a starting point. You don't know where you're affecting the child because you don't know where the starting line is, and that is an critical error for anyone using the Montessori Method.

You'll know where you're starting and how an activity or interaction impacts the child and whether it was positive or negative for that child. These eight stages of observation break down the key points in watching and following children, and it can drastically affect how you engage with them.

Stage One: When giving a lesson, you have the illusion of concentration. You may have a high level of awareness – but it's not actual observation.

Stage Two: Mobile observation. You aren't trying to give a lesson or teach something, but instead are watching on the move. The struggle here is that you don't have context for the activity you might interrupt, and any redirection or interruption you do give is not heeded because the child knows you're on the move. "Why stop what I'm doing when she's not coming back for a while?"

Stage Three: Taking a post. Understanding you have to stop walking and give a few moments for observation. This often results in a ton of frustration because you're "watching" but only taking note of things that bother you, or cultivating internal criticism or correction that builds up into stress.

Stage Four: Sitting and intervening. You know that mobile observation doesn't work, and taking a post resulted in frustration, so now you're telling children to come to you when you see something you don't like.

Stage Five: "Stink-eye" or using a disapproving look to "intervene" instead of physically or verbally intervening.

Stage Six: The "feeling good" stage. Children are coming to you with questions and demands, and you're responding.

Stage Seven: The "almost there" stage. A favorite Disney number, and the last stretch of getting used to observation: you're almost there. In this stage of observation, they can see you, you can see them, and they know you're there to watch, not interact. But you still give in to some questions and acknowledge issues when they arise.

Stage Eight: Observe as an observer. You're not interrupted, either because the child knows not to interrupt or because you're not acknowledging the interruption.

Step One: Sit and Watch

The Montessori method adopts the same techniques of observation that scientists use in field studies. You want to observe your child in their habitat with no interruptions and no interjections. Occasionally, if safety seems to be an issue, then it is time to interject. When we ran through the eight stages of observation, that is the natural progression of someone going from an unskilled or untrained level of observing to a skilled and well-honed observer.

Sitting and watching is difficult, especially for parents. The Montessori method excels in classrooms and learning centers because the adults there don't have the same attachment as you do. They may still love the children or find them fascinating. But, as parents, we feel the need to jump in when we see the child doing something that we believe is wrong. This can be playing with a toy so it wasn't intended by the manufacturer, or something outside of social norms. So, yes, it is challenging to sit and remain motionless, but the first stage of observation calls for that.

While you are sitting and watching, your body may seem emotionless and detached, but your mind should be outstandingly busy. Often, Montessori teachers note that observation is one of the most mentally demanding parts of their day.

Here are a few things that you'll want to remember or think through as you are beginning your observations:

- How often did you want to interrupt your child?
- Would that/those interruption(s) have been necessary?
- How did the child continue after hanging back or hesitating?
- What is the child exploring or trying to accomplish with their task?
- How often did you stop yourself from saying, *hey, don't,* or *no?*

These areas of interest are the biggest point of focus for parents of toddlers and babies. Toddlers are in a state of constant learning, and when we interject or step in and say no, then we're breaking that learning process. By sitting back for a while and watching how your child handles disappointment, frustration, curiosity, and other factors you might have stepped in on, you'll learn that they can do a lot. And they can do a lot that is still within the general social norms.

If you're not sure where to start, then break down your observations into a more structured analysis.

Those who are new to observing and maybe have a problem sitting still for long periods, can take a more analytical approach. Although eventually, you must give it go, you can start by taking notes. Use a small notepad and pen to keep a tally of how often you wanted to interrupt your child. Maybe take a few brief notes about how your child responded in different situations, and what areas of the room kept their interest for longer periods.

Step Two: Repeat Observations in Different Parts of the Home

Most children spend a fair amount of time in their bedroom, nursery, or maybe a shared area such as a living room. However, you may notice that their interests peak in the kitchen or even the bathroom. These are great times to observe as you can explore new interactions that might not be available in their normal play area.

Observation works best when observing the child at observation stage 7 or 8 in various elements. You might schedule observations, or observe when the moment strikes. Trying to ensure that you're not observing your child only in one environment, and only when they're doing one or two activities.

You also want the opportunity to see how well they function in different environments. It's a good way to test some of your elements in the environment. Observing your child in the kitchen can help you know if they can easily access all of their utensils or easily get up to wash their hands. Watching them in the bathroom or a bedroom can help you know what they can and can't access while playing or exploring.

Try to observe in each room of your home and outdoors. Parks or even just the backyard are great areas for observation. You know that for the sake of safety, you're keeping a very close eye on them. But at the same time, you can sit back and watch what elements of nature grab your child's attention. What are they fascinated with outside? Do they move near plant life and animals with ease or hesitancy? Is there a curiosity with sensory play, such as touching dirt or pulling leaves off of flowers?

Let your child loose and watch what they run to, what they explore, and where they spend their curiosity.

Step Three: Critically Reflect on Your Observations to Assess Readiness, Interests, and Needs

A ton of observation work is introspective. Understanding or noticing how often you want to interrupt, or jump can help you drastically change exactly how you interact with the child. It can also change how you perceive your environment. It is a challenge to understand an environment from the viewpoint of a toddler, but observations are the key to gaining the perception.

You may also notice clear cues that your child was hungry, thirsty, or wanted a buddy to play with. Without observation, that would have been easily overlooked. Often parents grow exceptionally frustrated at how children screech, whine or say "*uhn*" for everything. However, these are the flags or cues that parents often note they just don't understand. That ever eluding handbook for handling your baby, toddler, or child could be unlocked during observations.

A final purpose in observation is readiness assessment and interest assessment. Wondering what toys to get next, or if your child is ready to move on in their sensory play? Can they properly hold something steadily? Then it might be time to introduce water play. If they can suddenly pick up small items and aren't inclined to put them in their mouth, they could be ready for sorting activities.

Remember that observation periods should help you understand exactly where to go with the environment's direction, and how to help your child grow. This can help you assess when you feel the need to jump in and start back to see if perhaps the child can handle the situation independently. Observation is a critical point of the Montessori method. Most Montessori teachers acknowledge that if there were anything they could have more time doing, it would be doing observations.

Are you struggling to find time to fit in an observation period? Your alterations don't have to last for 30 minutes or an hour. You can take 10 or 15 minutes to sit and watch quietly. It is best if you can find a time when your child doesn't even see you. Passing by their room when they are playing and stopping in the doorway and just watching them play for 5 or 10 minutes is a great observation session.

Finally, let's end on a note of progress, not perfection. You need not have a perfect observation session. The idea is that you're starting your observations now, and in a few weeks or months, you'll have outstanding and rewarding observation sessions. Start now with what you have, and develop the observation skills so that further down the line, you can watch for 10 or 15 minutes, or even an hour, and walk away with significant information.

Chapter 5: Setting Up Your Montessori Home

Through the first four chapters, you have seen a brief mention of environment. The environment or the prepared environment is a critical point in the Montessori method. There's the idea of an orderly environment, and that the environment itself should provide engagement and cultivate curiosity. But how do you make that happen? Before you can dive headlong into the Montessori method and lifestyle, you need to get your home in order. Your home may be impeccable right now, but it might not be right for the tiny human in your home. Your house can cater to both adults and children, and in doing that, you'll likely create a safer environment too.

There are near-endless ways to create a more Montessori home. A Montessori home should:

1. Incorporate lessons that involve movement and spark interest.
2. Involve children in building life skills.
3. Allow your child to make mistakes and correct the mistakes themselves.
4. Isolate skills and concepts to create a foundation of knowledge

5. Thoughtful design to foster independence.

With these ideas, you can take immediate action. You can walk into your living room and assess the space and probably pick out five or six things you could remove, move, or at least make safer. Because one of the primary driving forces within the Montessori method is an independent exploration, you generally want to reduce the number of times you have to say no or jump in to take something away from the child. This isn't necessarily about putting cabinet locks on and making it impossible for toddlers to turn doorknobs. There is basic safety. Then there is the step of eliminating potential dangers by reducing potential harm.

While having a lock on the toilet seat might make sense if you're worried about your toddler getting into the toilet, the Montessori home looks at ways that parents intervene when they shouldn't have to because there's a reasonable alternative. For example, if you have glass knick-knacks out that you're constantly taking away from your child, they might serve better on a high shelf. Then replace those items with things that the toddler can pick up and touch and turn around and handle.

Assess Your Space

How do you get started? Start by assessing at face value. Sit down in the center of your living room or in your child's playroom or in your bedroom and look at the room from a seed of perspective. Remember that toddlers are typically much smaller than us, and they can see and get into things that never thought as an issue. That is until they pick it up, and we see them with it, and now we have to tell them "*no*" or "*stop.*" You know the drill.

Start in each room by sitting and looking through the things that your toddler could and probably will get into. Then take a minute to look at all the things they can't reach. What items up high that could pique their curiosity and possibly Inspire climbing? Think through and identify a few items that your child can pick up and play with or get into without interjection.

Finally, look at the practical elements of the space. Does your toddler have somewhere comfortable to sit or to lounge in your living room? Can they get onto their bed, or do they need help? Can they access drawers that contain their items, such as their clothing or toys?

Room by Room Montessori Style

Let's go through each room and assess what they can or should look like. Many Montessori schools look very similar because some foundational elements make it easy to recreate each room with a Montessori aesthetic.

Kitchen

The kitchen is a big room for Montessori parents and households that adopt the Montessori method. Maria Montessori emphasized that life skills are vital, and we should start life-skill development as early as possible. That means learning to cook, clean up, wash your hands, and organize or put things. This development need not happen exclusively in the kitchen, but the kitchen will be an important room for helping your toddler develop very basic life skills.

To get started, you can bring a stepladder into the kitchen. A step ladder will give your child access to the sink and a better view of the counter. If your child is tall and a simple step stool will do then, that's fine, but a step ladder gives them a little more height.

Then look at the tools and items that your child will use. Toddlers usually have their own set of utensils, plates, bowls, cups, and even snacks. You can put all of your toddler's kitchen items in a drawer on a pantry shelf they can easily access. It is beneficial to do this as most children will identify this accessibility as a better way of communication for being hungry or thirsty. Instead of throwing a tantrum or having trouble communicating their needs, they will often revert to going to the kitchen and getting a plate or getting a cup to acknowledge their fundamental need for food or a drink.

Putting their utensils and kitchen items where they can reach also encourages them to put away their own items. When you're unloading the dishwasher or the drying rack, you can hand them their utensils and plates so they can put them away.

As you introduce cleaning, the kitchen plays a very important role. Most people keep their cleaning products there, and you can do that for your toddler. Having a washcloth, and maybe a spray bottle of water with a lemon rind can make them part of the cleaning process. You can also have a small broom and dustpan available, so that when they drop something, they can quickly get their cleaning items and pick up after themselves. For most toddlers, this is a game, and it's a very fun one because they're mimicking something they've seen you do a thousand times that they've never had the tools to do themselves.

Bedroom/Nursery

Although every other room in the house needs to be accessible and easily usable for adults, a toddler's bedroom or nursery should care more for small hands and small stature. Consider making all toys and supplies available at a toddler's level, always keep their eye level in mind, and give consideration towards their natural inclination to pick up and touch, throw, and generally make a mess. When you place items at their eye level, it also makes it easier to engage them with cleaning activity.

One of the first things to tackle in the toddler's bedroom or nursery, or any room where they spend the most time, is to reduce stimuli. Too many posters, ribbons, decorations, and similar things can pull attention into too many directions at once. Your toddler needs to be engaged and to keep busy, but they shouldn't be overwhelmed.

Now, for art supplies, you can always refer to washable markers, washable crayons, and even Crayola's Color Wonder supplies, which are great as they don't mark on anything other than the special paper. Paint and other messy supplies that you might not want to leave out in the nursery or bedroom can come out during observation periods.

You can also encourage self-care by keeping most things available at their highest that you might otherwise put up higher. Clothes are the primary example here; when a child has access to their wardrobe, then they can pick what they like, and it might be a mess at first, but eventually, they'll lose interest in pulling out their clothes.

Here is a checklist for the bedroom or nursery:

- Keep clothes, toys, and items at toddler level.
- Focus on keeping child-sized furniture with a place for them to sleep, sit, and play.
- Possibly bring in a hand washing station.
- Use low shelves so everything is present and available, rather than drawers.
- Use clear buckets or cubbies to store similar items (blocks, sorting items, etc.).
- Make a system for cleaning or putting away items that even a toddler can understand.

Living Room

Keep some toys or interesting objects out and available at your toddler's reach. Think of items that can always be in the living room and are easy to put away. These items should still offer comfort and engagement. Typically pretend-play items are best for the living room because there are not usually multiple parts, and you can put them all together in one bucket or cubby.

Also, make sure that your little one has space. Consider a small chair for them or an area where they can lounge, especially if they haven't mastered climbing up onto the couch yet. You can also use a specific rug or a play rug to help acknowledge that they also have a space in the living room.

The living room is one of the biggest challenges for reducing interventions. Unlike in the kitchen where you'll constantly watch them, the living room offers enough safety for you to do another task or relax for a moment. Until that moment end because they start pulling down picture frames. Focus on safety and accessibility. Anchor furniture, including TVs, and move dangerous items out of reach or out of the room. Then, look at items you simply don't want them getting into, such as photo albums or meaningful knick-knacks. You might swap out outlets for toddler-safe or "safety" outlets.

The living room should be a place for everyone, and that means your toddler too. Now, they'll grow up quickly, so it's not like moving things to a high-shelf means they'll never see the light of day again. As your children get older, you can relax as they play with items you don't want to be damaged, broken, or lost. Trust is a big element in Montessori, especially as they grow, but at a young age, safety should come first, and you might not want things lost to a tantrum.

Bathroom

The bathroom is another spot with lots of dangers that most people just keep their children away from. It would be easier if your child were only allowed into the bathroom for a bath, using the restroom, and brushing their teeth. However, they also need to wash their hands, and having this as an "off-limits" room in the house is a recipe for potty-training disaster and many tantrums.

To make the bathroom more toddler-friendly:

- Have a step stool or step ladder so they can see and use the sink on their own.
- Use pitchers, plungers, and plastic tubes to promote pouring activities in the tub.
- Encourage bathtub play for sensory development.

What About the Overarching Basics?

There are overarching basics. Keep decor simple and engaging but not distracting. Use rugs on hard flooring, they're great for sensory development, but it's also useful because children will gravitate toward rugs for floor play. Make sure there are accessible items in every room that your child uses for playtime. Encourage them to explore while also maintaining safety with basic child-safety tools.

Wait, don't you need educational materials on every wall? What about the hand washing station in every room? In Montessori classrooms, these make sense, and you can put items up, but you need not make every room in your house look like it belongs in a Montessori center. Your home is also a living environment. In Montessori classrooms and homes, minimalism is a common theme; fewer things, but higher importance on the thoughtfulness of those things and how they are presented.

Chapter 6: Coordination and Sensory Activities

Babies start exercising their coordination of large muscle groups as early as four months old. From that age forward, they develop gross motor skills and fine motor skills, and this is done through coordination activities. A lot of these come up in every day-style child's play. We see kids running in parks, playing soccer, and pulling apart Legos. However, with the Montessori method in mind, there is a way to establish coordination and sensory activities within the toddler's environment to promote positive interaction. You shouldn't have to get up and say, "Hey, let's go outside and kick a ball around." Instead, your child should have access to all the other tools or toys that promote coordination development and sensory building.

Coordination and Sensory in Montessori

What is the Montessori method regarding coordination and sensory play, and how does that help develop muscles and memory? While sensory activities are fun and interesting, they also promote exploration and investigation. You'll notice after some time of working with different sensory activities that your child will begin to turn to the scientific method. They begin by observing, they will estimate what should happen after a certain action, they will experiment, and, after a while, they will draw their own conclusions.

We also know that purposeful sensory development helps build motor skills and nerve connections within the brain. Sensory play also links directly to language development and scientific thinking or problem-solving.

Developing better coordination helps toddlers understand and address problems that involve picking objects up and moving them. Coordination helps children understand how to minimize conflict, understand spatial recognition, and eventually helps them handle daily activities faster. You will sit around waiting forever for your child to put on their own shoes if they haven't properly mastered finger coordination. These coordination activities can do a lot more than what is initially seen. Give them a chance and have fun while you're doing interacting with your child. A lot of these activities do call for interaction by the parent or humble teacher.

Think Beyond the Go-To Activities

We have a ton of fun and engaging activities you can do with a toddler as young as 18-months-old. It might seem that some of these are very advanced, and you can acknowledge that through observations. Even if some of these activities seem beyond your child's immediate development stage, give them a shot and see if they're willing to participate and engage.

Our first activity turns a lot of heads for parents. Catching and throwing it seems like something a five or six-year-old should do. However, many two-year-old's can catch and throw well. Let's get into these activities.

Catch and Throw

Underhand, overhand, from the side, rolling across the floor, you can catch and throw in almost any way possible. It is fun, builds coordination, and there are a lot of endless opportunities to be silly. However, there are a few ways to really amp up this activity.

Consider having a variety of ball sizes as the different sizes will exercise different portions of muscles in your child's hands. If your child doesn't have the catch-and-throw idea down, start with a beach ball. They are light and easy to pick up with two hands. They're also super easy to throw overhead. Then your child gets the big reward of the ball going far because of its weight and can execute a 'proper' throw.

If you don't want to encourage throwing indoors, you might use soft-hit or squishy balls. Otherwise, keep the balls outside for catching and throwing.

Walk with a Lemon

Walking with an egg balanced on a spoon is a favorite of holiday and office parties. However, your slightly less coordinated little person at home can reconstruct this game. Give them a head start on the office parties. To play this game, set a starting point and a finish line. One great way to set these points is to use masking tape, Washi tape, or just simply place start and finish line items on the floor.

The "walk with a lemon" game can work in two ways. First, the toddler can simply hold the spoon while balancing a lemon and walking from the start to the finish point. Second, the toddler can hold the spoon in their mouth. There are a few things to remember if you challenge your toddler to walk with the lemon balancing on a spoon held in their mouth. First, try to avoid using metal spoons for their teeth. Second, use the smallest lemon you can find or fall back to limes because they are much lighter.

The best part of using a lemon rather than an egg is the peace of mind regarding cleaning up. There is nothing about this activity you should have to clean up. Your toddler should be able to return the lemon to its place, put the spoon back, or toss the spoon out if it was plastic, and pick up the start and finish line areas.

Container Bowling

How many Tupperware containers do you have in your cupboard? Tupperware, stacking containers, and even plastic cups all make great pins for bowling. All you need for this activity are a couple of somewhat stackable items and a ball that is heavy or large enough to knock the items over or out of the way.

You may notice that toddlers set up bowling differently than we know the game. Many toddlers will set up their bowling space how we might see the traditional carnival game of knocking over pins or bottles. This setup is acceptable and offers a bigger reward for tipping over items with a successful bowl.

Typically, expect your child to get wildly creative with their bowling setups. It's a great reason why this activity is so great for coordination. They're not just knocking over pins, but also taking the time to place them strategically or stack them upwards.

If you're looking to put together this game with just items from around the house, consider using disposable cups, either Styrofoam or plastic. Your child will have fun stacking the cups up or placing them in a bowling setup, and then they can do almost any size ball, and the cups will tip over.

Stack Containers

The Pink Tower is a well-known Montessori tool. However, you need not buy specific tools to get started with this activity. If you're trying to gauge how interested your toddler is in stacking and similar coordination activities, use items from around the house. Not only will this help build your child's coordination, but it promotes creativity.

How many cups can they stack upward? How many Tupperware containers will nest inside each other? Can they stack books? Is it possible that their animal figurines will stack up too? Stacking containers or nearly any kitchen or bathroom storage device can help toddlers grasp the concept of coordination and facial recognition.

They must explore and decide for themselves whether an item will stay stacked on top of the other item or not.

A final note on stacking containers. If you're worried about the toddler stacking things too high, or using items that may be heavy, then you're sitting right there observing. You don't want to interject before it's necessary. This activity is such a great opportunity to watch your child go through the scientific process and use household items to cultivate creative coordination play.

Dry Pouring

Dry pouring is an absolute favorite among Montessori parents and teachers. It is as simple as gathering beans, rice, pasta, sand, moon sand, or even dirt from outside. Because this activity has so many variations, we will include a few tips and tricks to help make it a little more fun too.

So, what is dry pouring? Dry pouring is an exercise or activity that allows the toddler access to a dry material they can scoop and then pour from one container into another. Some parents use sheet pans, pots, storage containers, or buckets. If you have a few buckets from summer, the pails intended for beach use, those are excellent for this activity.

How to Color Beans, Pasta, or Rice for Dry Pouring

- Divide the desired beans, pasta, or rice between three to seven sandwich bags.
- Drop a few drops of food coloring into each bag (you can go from primary colors to the full rainbow). A few drops go a long way!
- Wait for 24-hours for the beans, pasta, or rice to dry.
- Place the beans or rice onto a sheet pan or in bowls.

Moon sand is also excellent for this activity because the child can pour and move the sand in clumps or in its sandy form.

How to Make Moon Sand

1. Place 8 cups of flour into a large bowl or container.

2. Create a crater in the middle of the flour.

3. Pour 1 cup of baby oil into the crater.

4. Mix the oil and flour in a churning and kneading motion

In its final form, the moon sand will still look suspiciously like flour. However, as soon as your little one gets their hands on it, the sand will clump up. Great for pouring and watching something change from an almost rock shape into sand again.

When you're looking for pouring tools, you can go to the tried-and-true measuring cups. However, you can also use sand shovels, bath rinses, spoons, ladles, containers, and cups.

The element of coordination here is to get a generally large amount of the item from one container into another container. This activity is great for outdoor play. Set a plastic planter of dirt in front of your child and watch as they methodically scoop it with a tool and pour it onto the ground. Easy to clean, and most young children will have a prolonged interest in this activity.

Sorting Items

Montessori teachers know and love sorting activities. These activities are straightforward and definitely something you can do at home with little effort. You can use the same beans or rice you had for pouring, for sorting. Making big batches of colored beans, rice, or pasta is an excellent way to switch from one activity to another. Dye your beans, rice, or different pasta colors.

Place the items on a sheet pan or mixed in a bowl. If you're mixing items together in a bowl, you might use beans and pasta rather than rice. Then have your toddler sort these items by color. Give them the appropriate goals for the number of colors that they're sorting. Allow them to develop their fine motor skills and coordination to pick up these small items and drop them into a bowl. These activities are a great opportunity to build pincer grip strength. You'll notice that your toddler naturally tries to pick up these smaller items between their thumb and forefinger.

One element of sorting activities that stands out from some of these other coordination activities is the focus. Toddlers find bowling and musical instruments engaging. However, sorting items calls for more focus. They have to not only engage tactically but also think strategically about where to place the item and if it's in the correct bowl.

One of the more famous Montessori tools or toys is the Sorting Bears. You can now find sorting bears not only in bear shape but as dinosaurs, chickens, trains, and more. This toy often comes away with around 50 differently colored small-shaped items. Then there are seven cups, each a different color of the rainbow. Usually, with tongs or their fingers, that child will pick up each little bear or dinosaur and place it in the cup that matches its color. You need not invest in this toy right away, or even. If you would rather use household items, that is fine, and some Montessori teachers promote the use of alternative items. If you're stretching your creativity to put together these activities, the child will see that resourcefulness and mimic it.

String Beads or Pasta

A little yarn, large beads, or large size tube-shaped pasta can keep your little one entertained for quite a while. However, this activity can go wrong quickly. When stringing beads or pasta, you need to think about the environment and the tools available. Two-year-old's are typically far past putting things in their mouth. However, even children as old as four or five can do this thinking it is funny, and they're oblivious of the choking hazard.

Yarn is typically better than fine string or even embroidery thread because it's easier for small hands to handle. When looking for beads, you want something larger than Perler Beads. Many parents using Montessori as a model will use large rigatoni or penne pasta. Using pasta can also help children learn to control their pincer grip or their palm grip in that if they drip too hard, they will crush the pasta. Only use pasta in its dry form.

When setting up this activity, you'll want to put restrictions in place. For example, take the yarn down to the table, floor, or play area. You might also create a small enough piece of yarn that the toddler can't wrap it around anything they shouldn't.

Let's make a Deal

Is it possible that your child can learn coordination and develop their decision making? Absolutely! The 'let's make a deal game' is pretty fun, and you can use this game as early as six-months-old. Although six months is a little young regarding toddler discipline, this can help set the stage for decision-making and compromise.

There are a few elements of daily life to consider when putting together this activity. First, this activity requires the participation of the humble teacher or a Montessori parent. This activity does not count as observation, although you'll probably walk away with some good insight into your child's decision-making abilities and personal preferences. Second, you can tailor this game toward things you know your child likes or present new items. Finally, you want to keep a distraction-free environment and try to play this game somewhere there aren't other items your child may want.

So, how does this work?

- Step one, sit your child or toddler down and hand them two items.
- Step two, hold up a new item in front of your child and request they exchange something they're already holding for the new item.
- Step three, repeat the process with new items until your child loses interest.

Now the instructions are straightforward, but they rarely account for some serious deviations happen. As a toddler, your child may cleverly refuse to give up any items and instead take multiple items into their arms or set them in their lap. Mostly, this is acceptable. Ideally, you want them to exchange one item they already had for a new item. However, your child will eventually run out of space and have to start giving-up items to take new items.

Or you could take a different approach and acknowledge that everything is an even exchange. The child cannot have the new until they decide which one they will give up. Whatever approach you choose is up to you; just remember that consistency and fairness are vital to children.

The other issue that comes up during this game is the child not wanting to give up any item and has no interest in the offered item. When the child shows no interest in the offered item, it is okay just to set that item to the side. When you send items to the side, it is an indicator that your child just has zero interest in that thing. Now, because of changing interest, the Montessori parents will use this activity to gauge interest. They may use only kitchen items during one game, and then on a different day, use items that the child often uses. You may do this activity outside and offer different plants or different outdoor toys.

Everyday Instruments

Most adults have seen or heard of very young children or toddlers banging on pots and pans. That is essentially what you're recreating with this activity. Pots, pans, Tupperware, rubber bands, paper towel tubes, and many other household items produce music or at least sound.

When setting up this activity, you might wrap a few thick rubber bands around an open-container or bowl. You might provide a set of wooden spoons and pans that your child can run with or paper towel tubes of different lengths they can blow through.

You can also turn to standard instruments. Recorders, drums, sound tubes, maracas, and tambourines are excellent toddler instruments. Almost every instrument requires proper holding or engagement of the hands and one way or another. Drums evidently call upon coordination, but the sound tubes are an excellent Montessori tool because of how they create different sounds depending on where they are struck.

For these activities, if you are trying to lead a lesson, ask the child to produce different sounds using one instrument. For example, you might shake out one beat with a maraca and ask them to make a different rhythm.

Water Painting

Water painting is an absolute favorite, especially for parents that don't want the mess of painting. You need a stack colored paper only, or butcher's paper, and water. Children can water paint with their fingers, paint brushes, foam brushes, or pom-poms. Pom-poms are a fun variation; they clearly produce different size droplets of water and develop the pincer grip in toddlers.

What's water painting, you might ask? They paint over something you've already put onto the paper. It is a great way to promote tracing and advanced coordination or encourage the development of their alphabet. You can make simple lines, wavy lines, letters, numbers, and much more.

Button Tracing

Similar to water painting, button tracing is a low-mess activity that focuses on coordination development. With button tracing, you'll want to have a variety of button sizes, but nothing so small they could be a choking hazard. Then you must sit down before you start the activity to make a few basic shapes.

To get started with button tracing, take construction paper or printer paper, and create a few designs. Start with only four or five pages. On each page, you can put more than one design, but it's better to keep their focus on one thing when they're new to this activity.

On a single page, you might create a dotted line version of a letter, number, or image. You can create the general outline of a smiley-face or a tree, and then I have a toddler use buttons to cover up the dotted lines and complete the image. Button tracing develops pincer grip, spatial recognition, and sliding.

Chapter 7: Helping Around the House

When your house is set up as a Montessori environment, then you may find it easier to get help around the house. Toddlers naturally want to be helpful, and they want to be around the adults in their life. Although a lot of the Montessori method revolves around children learning from similarly aged peers, there's much they can only learn from you. Cleaning up around the house is a basic life skill, and it's one that every adult needs.

As a bonus for parents, getting a little extra help around the house, but the chores should be micro-chores. You wouldn't ask your toddler to tackle the dishes by themselves. You're also not expecting them to dedicate more than one or two minutes to any particular activity. Sure, some of these will take you a while to complete, but by offering to let them help, they can come and go in the activity as their interest spikes and wanes.

Toddlers can hardly ever accomplish these things with perfection, especially on the first try. But implementing these can drastically reduce your stress in the long-term. Not only because you're getting help with household tasks, but because you know that your child can confidently handle these tasks and they are learning life skills.

What Can Your Child Actually Do?

So, what can your toddler do around the house? The bigger question is actually what they can't do. Your toddler can help you unload the dishwasher, put their plate into the dishwasher, help with laundry, help care for household plants, clean up their toys, pick up small messes, wipe up spills, and even meal prep. A lot of the restrictions we put on small children are simply because we know we can do these tasks faster and with greater effectiveness. However, when we involve these children early, they can quickly improve their skills in these tasks and provide greater help at younger ages. These are life skills that they will have to learn eventually, so why not start early?

Dishes

There are always some restrictions. As Maria Montessori preached, freedom with restrictions is the ideal situation for toddlers and young children. The dishwasher is a great example. If your toddler is helping to unload the dish drying rack or the dishwasher, then you clearly wouldn't be handing them knives to put away. You may also avoid handing over heavy casserole dishes. But they can have a grand time stacking together Tupperware and putting away spoons. When instructing how to help unload the dishwasher, you can teach a toddler how to carry things with two hands and how to ask for help when there's something they can't reach.

Laundry

With handling laundry, there' are a lot of opportunities. Not only can they help put away folded laundry, but they can help sort clothes into piles. They can help by sorting towels, bedding, light-colored clothing and whites, and dark colors. They can also help her clean laundry out of the dryer. If you have a front-loading dryer, this is much easier, but you can still hand them clean items from a top-loading dryer and ask them to put them in the laundry basket.

Cleaning Up Their Toys

Many parents don't ask their children to pick up their own toys until they're four or five years old. Your toddler can learn to clean up their toys as early as one-year-old. The way they will learn is by watching you. You are modeling behavior and constantly asking for support or help. We covered that toddlers love to help, and they also don't like having their things touched.

When you pick up their toys, you can instigate them to help you. Always start by asking for help and acknowledging that it's their mess or their toys.

If your child has reached the age where they like things a particular way, you can make it a game. You can pick up an item and say it loudly that you will put it somewhere it doesn't belong. Then, start walking toward the wrong area where you intend to put down this toy and watch as your toddler springs into action to correct you. You can also play the fool and act as though you don't know where anything goes. You can pick up an item and ask, "oh, does this go in the garage?" or "I think this goes in your sister's room." Toddlers love to correct adults when they know that things work in a specific way. Giving them that opportunity helps build skills for knowledge sharing, and it means you can sit in one spot on the floor, and they'll do most of the actual cleaning.

Small Messes and Spills

Small spills and messes happen every day. If your child is new to using an open container rather than a sippy cup or bottle, they may even happen multiple times per hour. Together you can get past crying over spilled milk when you know that you have help cleaning it up. Arm your toddler with a small stack of washcloths in the kitchen, bathroom, and wherever they play the most.

That way, when a spill happens, they can grab a washcloth, because they know where they are, and immediately soak up the liquid.

With messes, you may have to give a little more guidance. Messes such as crumbles from food might require a vacuum or a broom and dustpan. You can get a child-sized broom and dustpan so the toddler can sweep on their own. They may not always do a good job; they probably will usually do a very good job, but it doesn't make the mess worse. You allow them to try to clean up the mess, and the reward of helping.

Meal Prep and Cooking

Do you remember how old you were when you started cooking? Most of us don't start actively cooking until we move out on our own. However, you can involve your toddler in the cooking process at a young age. Toddlers are excellent at peeling oranges, washing vegetables, and pouring in the pre-measured elements of a meal.

Evidently, there are a wide variety of dangers in the kitchen. From boiling water to knives, it seems as though even the simplest snacks can present immediate peril. Most of this is our own concern because there is a wide variety of activities you can do as long as they have your supervision. If you need to mix or stir something, ask your toddler. They can at least try.

The safest activities in the kitchen for toddlers involve washing vegetables and fruit, peeling fruit with their hands, not with a peeler, and stirring mixtures together. When stirring, they can use a spoon, whisk, or fork, and they often do well. If it seems as though asking your toddler for help in the kitchen means the task taking forever, remember that their short attention spans will quickly have them out of the kitchen. Most toddlers are very happy to find somewhere quiet to play while you continue cooking after only a few minutes of offering their help. There is a type of security that comes with knowing they can return to your side if they want to, but most of the time, they'd rather play independently.

How are "Chores" a Part of Your Child's Montessori Experience?

Chores aren't necessarily the choice word used among the Montessori Community, but let's be honest; it is what it is. Even as adults, we know that doing the dishes and folding laundry are chores. However, we can reframe this unpleasant task for children. Not only can micro chores with your children be fun, but they help to build a respectful relationship. You know that you don't like doing these things, but your child doesn't know these are unpleasant things yet. If more adults worked with teaching these household duties are not chores but instead part of a group contribution to maintaining a proper household, we might have happier adults.

So how do we do this, and how are these household duties part of the Montessori experience? It always starts with tools and invitations. Your toddler cannot hold a full-size broom and use it effectively. To invite your child to help sweep, then get them a tool that's their size. Don't rush out and buy a bunch of household cleaning utensils that are child size. Much of the cleaning can be done purchasing nothing because you can use paper towels, washcloths, spray bottles, and sponges for the majority of your household cleaning.

So, once you have the tools, or have found that item that your toddler can easily handle, you can move into the invitation. The invitation is your extension to your toddler that you will do an activity, and they are welcome to do it with you. This is as easy as asking for help. You might say, "I'm going to get the laundry; can you help me fold?" With the right framing, you can present this as something you'll do together rather than something you will do, and they can leave you alone or be in your way.

Now we mentioned earlier that help us love helping, but toddlers are also destructive even if it's unintentional. How many parents have folded and stacked laundry only to turn around and find their two-year-old throwing folded items up into the air? Even if not every parent has experienced this, I'm willing to bet there are a fair few who know the situation. Pay close attention to the language you use as you follow up on that invitation. Instead of saying get out of the way, you might say excuse me. If they miss a spot, instead of saying, "Oh, you missed blah blah," it might sound better than, "Can I try now?"

The Montessori experience always comes back to freedom with restrictions. The fact is: *the house will not maintain itself.* Another fact is that no single adult should be exclusively responsible for cleaning up after multiple people. Your toddler lives in the house and must eventually learn to help maintain the house. This need not be unpleasant, and don't call them chores, and it need not be a grudging obligation for anyone in the house. When coming back to freedom with restrictions, your toddler has the freedom to help you and to contribute to the house, and in doing that, they'll be a bigger part of the household. The Restriction is that when the environment is not clean or orderly, everyone in the house feels it. Someone has to clean, and if your toddler is choosing not to participate or not to engage in the invitation, then they will find out when they attempt to engage you, and you're doing these activities. At that point, you're busy.

Show, Show, Show, Then Observe, and Always Involve

"Tell me, and I forget, teach me, and I may remember, involve me, and I may learn." This is a well-known quote from Benjamin Franklin. Although he was born long before Maria Montessori introduced the concept of involvement and engagement to children, he had the right idea. You can show and tell your toddler. However, it's only through involving your child that they'll effectively learn the life skills necessary to maintain a house of their own someday.

As a toddler, you're not expecting them to keep the cogs of the household turning. You're simply expecting them to get involved and to help in a very small capacity. You are not assigning chores to your toddler. You're also not giving them a job to do on a regular basis. Through using Maria Montessori teaching, we know that modeling the behavior we want from our children is the best way to produce desirable results. We know that even when they don't take up our invitation to help in cleaning up if we do it, then they'll see it is part of a daily routine.

Show your toddler how you do each activity, and maybe even narrate the process. Then when they do want to help, take a moment to observe their actions. It's always a benefit to watch how toddlers and children have picked up on so much by just watching us work. But it is not enough to show your toddler and then to observe when they're in action. You need to continue that open line of communication and involvement.

Some parents schedule time for cleaning and acknowledge to their toddler or child that they're welcome to help. Other parents use little moments of time to pick up and again invite their toddlers to help. Either method works. You can be firm or flexible. The important thing here isn't how you do it. It's about involving them in the process and keeping that involvement consistent. Practical life is a driving force among Montessori parents and educators. These are also parts of everyday life, from picking up clothes off the ground to returning objects to their home. They must develop life skills and helping out around the house is a great way to start introducing these elements of practical life.

Chapter 8: Music, Movement, and Montessori

One famous Maria Montessori quote addresses the topic of music directly. It states, "There should be music in the child's environment, just as there does exist in the child's environment spoken speech. In the social environment, the child should be considered, and music should be provided." Maria Montessori states a direct correlation between music, movement, and development. Music is, in itself, a language. However, unlike English, Italian, Spanish, French, or any of the other languages we speak, music brings movement with it. Music ties communication with our physical bodies and these activities explore music and movement so it fits into the Montessori model.

Some of these activities and methods of interaction pull directly from age-old Montessori teaching. Others rely on newer information and tactics and introducing music to toddlers. Either way, music is a great way to have fun.

What Children Learn from Music and Movement

Music improves literacy, numerical sense, sensory development, enhances moods, and physical coordination. Music is also a critical way to build a toddler's vocabulary. Basically, if you're looking to bring the Montessori discipline into your home, music should play a big role in that plan. Music can be a way to redirect children toward positive interactions, or used as a mood lifter, it can make meltdowns easier to handle.

We've known that music has these abilities even at a young age since the time of Plato. Plato said this on children and music:

> *"I would teach children music, physics, and philosophy; but most importantly, music, for the patterns in music and all the arts are the keys to learning."* - Plato

Music provides a delicate balance between mathematics and the physical realm. It accomplishes that balance while fostering creativity and sensory exploration. The experimentation and creation processes of engaging in musical activity are beyond value. It accelerates brain development and sensory development.

Because of children naturally mimicking our moves and behaviors, we can all teach without providing "instruction. Through doing this, our children will watch and model our motions and habits. When building up their interest in music, you only have to start by presenting the tools, resources, and of course, source material.

One important element to address is that don't push kids into sheet music. Although many regarded Mozart as a prodigy, it is more likely that his father, a trained musician, and composer, pushed formal training on him. Don't worry about formal training just yet. Always remember that Montessori teaching and models focus on the child finding what interests them and exploring that interest freely and creatively.

When Did Music Become Part of the Montessori Model?

Auditory sensory development was one of the first major changes that Maria Montessori made after observing children. Children in traditional schools were subjected to different visual stimuli, but the auditory stimulus was significantly lacking. Musical activities were promoted through the years, such as nursery rhymes, bells, easy to handle instruments, and dance. Interpreting music and movement not only addresses the need for auditory sensory development but for developing coordination and gross and fine motor skills.

As with all things of the Montessori model, through the refining and introducing auditory stimulus, Maria Montessori ensured that music and movement created a cooperative learning environment. All the activities mentioned here help create a cooperative and well-organized environment while also promoting independent work and instruction.

Maria Montessori recognized that having music around, with or without words, can help children identify sound patterns and learn because of repetition. Music also helps children learn anticipation and to predict what will come next because of patterns in that repetition. Children that have frequent exposure to music master literacy and numeracy at much younger ages. When linking music with movement and dance, they can increase their skill level and abilities with strength, balance, and muscle development.

Early into developing the Montessori method, it was evident that children's natural love of music and making sound was an integral part of the learning experience.

How to Bring Music Into Your Home

Your home may already have a wealth of music involved. We all saw how quickly songs such as a baby shark took off, and it's evident that parents are still very involved in introducing nursery rhymes and sing songs to their children. However, it is a struggle to bring more music into the home and reduce time with the TV or a screen. Even with smash hits such as Baby Shark and nursery rhymes reimagined through animation with companies such as Super Simple Songs, the child is still in front of a screen.

One element of sensory development that Maria Montessori returned to repeatedly was that such development should attempt to focus on one sense at a time. If at all possible, reduce the time you promote music along with visual stimulus. Even just having music playing in the background can drastically change the mood and feeling of the environment.

Not every music activity has to eliminate screens, and not every music activity requires dance. But relying on activities that do involve movement (or an additional stimulus) can promote engagement with the child. Toddlers are not only naturally curious, but they're natural music makers.

We'll dive into specific activities, but for now, here are a few extremely easy ways to bring music into your home:

- Stream music or the radio whenever possible
- Leave out instruments frequently for interaction.
- Sing what you're doing (It's more common and less weird than you might think!) Really, just narrate what you do in a sing-song voice and listen to your toddler do the same.

When looking for ideas on streaming, you can always tune into a local classical channel or even your favorite radio station. If you use a streaming service, you might search for "happy songs," "toddler songs," or even "happy music." The music should serve as a stimulus, but also as a mood booster. Who doesn't want a happy toddler? Part of tapping into that happy toddler essence is preventive measures, and music could be the key to getting your toddler into a good mood early in the day.

Tools

You want a range of instruments, some that you may need to handle, and others that little hands can easily grasp and interact with daily. And you'll want, for a variety of reasons, a wide range of sounds. There are times when you might turn to softer instruments, but when the kids want to make big sounds. You should have both options available.

For many reasons, most parents do not want the Montessori bells in their homes. There is no blame or shame in not bringing the bells home. Some parents have created **DIY** Montessori bells and intentionally placed them outside. The Montessori bells are loud and not always pleasant. However, they provide a massive amount of opportunity for exploration within a scale. If you can bring the bells into your home, give them a chance.

Reference this list for possible music and movement tools to bring into your home:

- Xylophones or pentatonic metallophone
- Bongos or conga drums
- Shakers
- Castanets
- Jingle sticks
- Tambourine
- Ukulele
- Sound cylinders
- Tone blocks
- Rain sticks and thunder sticks

Get Toddlers Moving and Grooving with These Montessori Music and Dance Activities

Getting your toddler interested starts with the presentation. If you can, dedicate a shelf to musical items. That shelf should be at your child's level and then place each instrument in a basket or cubby. However, you might also put them all together in one box, or bring them out when you can have more noise in the house.

Once you decide how you'll display or provide the instruments, you can move onto some activities. Some of these are very simple, and others do provide instruction.

Singing Time

You can sing together or take turns. Singing time is a great opportunity to explore turn-taking. But it's also a great way to prompt memory. Start by humming the beginning to a familiar tune and then ask the child to sing the song. You can also use sing-along tracks where the music plays but not the lyrics. It's very much like karaoke.

You can initiate it with a familiar song and then move into singing songs that are new where they can grow their vocabulary and repertoire.

Coordinated Dance

You can accomplish coordinated dance time in a few ways. First, you can put on a YouTube video of a coordinated toddler dance or nursery song such as Baby Shark. Second, you can lead your toddler through dances you might already know, such as I'm a Little Tea Pot.

Coordinated dance should be the introduction to dancing. You might hand the reins over to your toddler once they seem to have it down.

Free Dance

Mats or rugs are excellent for free dance sessions. Set out a yoga mat or dedicate a rug to dancing. Turn on the radio and let them shake, bounce, and disco it out. The best way to conduct dancing activities is to model. The Montessori method relies heavily on the parent or teacher modeling the activity or the behavior. If you're looking for fun ways to connect with your toddler while still using the Montessori method, dancing is a great opportunity.

Walk the Line

You don't need Johnny Cash to walk the line, but walking the line is a fun activity specifically for classical music. Use tape (electrical tape is great for this) and put down one line on the ground. Your line can be straight, a circle, an ampersand, or even a treble clef if you want to get fancy.

Then play classical music and have them move along the line in response to the music. They can move to the beat, to the melody, or just in response to their emotions.

Songs that Engage Movement

Have you heard, "One Little Finger" or "Head Shoulders Knees and Toes?" If so, then you already know a few songs that engage movement. You can get your vibrant and unaware toddler to sing at the top of their lungs while also learning parts of the body and how to follow directions.

One of the major misconceptions in the Montessori Method is there should be no direction given. Even Montessori teachers seem to struggle with this concept as they offer advice such as, "I don't find myself giving instructions often," or "We let the children decide." The toddler can still decide if they want to participate or not, but it's okay to say, "*Watch mom/dad*" and then turn on the song or sing it and do the dance. They can participate or not.

These songs promote engagement, movement, interaction, and body awareness. They're also a ton of fun to do with your child. Music that engages movement isn't really the time for observations.

Try these songs:
- Itsy Bitsy Spider
- Baby Shark
- Stand Up, Sit Down
- This Little Finger
- Party Freeze Dance
- Wiggle It Dance
- The Airplane Song
- Five Little Monkeys

Look up the dance moves, but if you have access to the songs, you can always make up your own dances.

Musicians from Montessori Teaching

Musicians are well known for emerging from Montessori teaching. Unlike the prodigies of old, such as Mozart, these people weren't drilled with fundamental practices. Instead, it's about letting them explore, try new sounds, and learn the physical restrictions regarding music themselves.

Each musician received worldly accolades. Now, there's no guarantee that your child will become an international sensation in any genre. However, the time you spend with your child, allowing your toddler to explore music, can develop a lifelong passion. Music can drastically affect your child if you let it, and these famous people show just that.

Taylor Swift

The first of the Grammy award-winners on our list, Taylor Swift, is a household name. She was announced as country music's youngest-ever Entertainer of the Year and she attended the Alvernia Montessori School, in Berks County, PA. She's widely applauded Montessori teachings for young children and even donated directly to the Montessori school she attended.

Yo-Yo Ma

With 15 Grammy's, a National Medal of the Arts, and recognized as a child prodigy cellist, Yo-Yo Ma stands apart from many musicians. The reason for this? The ability to think outside of traditional definitions and restrictions in music by pursuing his own interest. As a United Nations Peace Ambassador, it's clear that the desire to continue growing and improving his versatility was nurtured early.

Joshua Bell

Award-winning violinist Joshua Bell was also involved in a cultural experiment, which became a Pulitzer prize-winning story. Internationally renowned, Bell began experimenting with music at three, and by four, was playing the violin. He started his education in the Montessori Method. Like many, at some point, he excelled and was placed into standard schooling. Bell's first record came out in 1988, and he is still creating music.

Beyonce Knowles

Beyonce started in Houston, Texas. During her career, she's won 22 Grammy's, appeared in Time Magazine's 100 most influential people in the world, and sold over 100 million records. Her love of music began early. At St. Mary's Montessori School in Houston, Knowles attended classes at a very young age. When she was seven, she won a talent show. She continued at St. Mary's Montessori until third grade and still credits the school for empowering her and fostering her lifelong love of music and learning.

Chapter 9: Learning New Skills the Montessori Way

Learning new skills, including the development of language, speech, reading, numerical sense, writing, and much more, is all possible through Montessori methods. These methods are helpful ways to not only make learning fun but to sneak it in through everyday activities. You won't have to sit your toddler down and say, "Well, today we're learning to write." Instead, the new skill will emerge rather naturally.

The ability to learn new skills and engage in new activities with confidence is one cornerstone of Montessori learning techniques. This factor is also what drives people toward the Montessori model. When you have toilet-trained, two-year-old's and three-year-old's that can write and spell their name, it's pretty impressive. Now, remember that Montessori doesn't advocate for comparing and contrasting children's development levels. Still, it's hard not to see the rampant success of skill building in the Montessori community.

Challenges Montessori Parents and Teachers Have Adjusting to New Skill Development Methods

We should spend at least a moment addressing the challenge that Montessori teachers and parents face. This is not the standard technique, and many adults have trouble allowing children to self-direct their early learning. The idea that reading, numerical sense, and language development can be self-taught or self-directed is foreign in our standard education system.

However, it is largely that predetermined or traditional education system causing these perception problems. Not only can children develop an interest in reading, language, and numbers on their own, but they can explore that interest avidly if they have the right tools. During Montessori observation, children may be better at directing the learning as they are naturally inclined to create games.

Learning number sense, learning to read, learning the alphabet, and learning to write can all be games present in the child's natural element.

Language and Speech Skills

Language and speech skills go back directly to the core of Montessori practice. A lot of the elements necessary to develop language and speech skills depend on classic Montessori tools. These tools can include sandpaper letters and phonetic letters or cards. Have the child lead and to offer Insight rather than correction. However, language is a particularly problematic subject within the English language.

English is a difficult language to tie directly to phonetic sounds. Much of our language has silent spellings and letters, which changes the core sound of the word away from its phonetic pronunciation. For example, "bear" does not sound like "b," "eh," ah," "rr," it sounds like "bare," and that's a different word. It seems like we're over-complicating the matter here, but giving children a real-life application of phonetics is simply done with sandpaper letters. Ask them to choose the letter that matches the sound you make.

Activity

Using sandpaper letters, read through a book, or go through a nursery rhyme. As you say a word or emphasize a sound, point to the letter that makes that same sound.

- "Ka" - C
- "Ba" - B
- "Da" - D

After you point it out to them for a while, your child will replicate your behavior. You may quickly notice they will happily lead this game on their own. They may even play it without you around, but giving them the basics or the fundamental elements is the jumping-off point they need.

What tools do you need for language and speech development? Try having these tools on hand:

- Moving alphabet
- Sandpaper letters
- Board books (your favorites are fine, embrace authors like Dr. Seuss or Eric Carle who evoke rhymes and repetition)
- Objects on flashcards or pictures on flashcards

Activity

A particularly fun activity is allowing the child to match an item to a picture card or flashcard. Give them a box or bucket of small items and a set of cards with things that match. A card with a ball, for example, would match the ball pit ball from the bucket. Your child can self-lead this activity. They may not start matching items, but give them some time, and they'll figure it out.

A variant of this activity provides them with a bucket of items and then use sandpaper letters. Then pick up an item. You can ask what sound matches this "Beee-ar" or "Zzzzebra"?

The first sound is important at first, but you can quickly revert to just saying the word how it comes naturally. Don't lead every activity like this, and you don't need to correct them if they say something a little off. If they're outright saying the wrong word, then feel free to say the correct word and show the correct movement to the sound.

Number Skills and Concept Development

Number skills actually come much more naturally to us than the traditional school system leads us to believe. It is through the rigidity of memorizing times tables and running mathematic drills that people feel they are inherently bad at math or that math is complex. In fact, number skills are some of the earliest skills we learn in terms of mental work. Not only can toddlers learn to count at a young age, but they also understand the value and comprehend the concepts of less and more.

These activities are engaging ways to get your child exercising their number sense without dragging them through a math lesson.

Activity

Snowflake cards are pretty easy to find, and you can easily make them yourself. Create or use cards with a few different snowflake designs, specifically those that have a different number of branches. Have two of each design.

Toddlers can match the cards or count the snowflake branches. After a while, you may notice your toddler arranging the cards in order from most to fewest branches or the other way around.

Activity

Deci-pockets are the open pocket tools that hang against the wall. Children or toddlers can handle their moving alphabet or moving numbers by moving them around on the wall within the deci-pocket.

For this activity, don't focus on getting the numbers in order straight away. Instead, focus on using the numbers to aid in nursery rhymes and small stories. You can use them to help your toddler follow along to rhymes such as, "5 little monkeys" or "5 little speckled frogs."

And you can use numbers in a story. You can make up stories, have your toddler make up stories, or simply go through your day. For example, you can start, "Today we woke up at eight," (then use the number eight in the deci-pocket) and follow up with, "*We will have a snack at ten.*" You can get elaborate by emphasizing the number of anything, really. "*You watched Tinkerbell and her five fairy friends.*" Or "*We bought one big jug of milk at the store.*"

Developing Writing Skills

Writing doesn't just include language. It also includes numbers. Some great Montessori tools come with developing writing skills, and they all are presented as games or fun activities.

There are activities to develop writing skills that happen both during the learning to write process and pre-writing. With pre-writing activities, you will focus on developing that pincer grip and hand movement. That often happens with wooden objects, stacking items, and nesting items.

To help develop a pincer grip, allow your child to use tweezers during sorting activities, or to hold standard size crayons or pencils. It may be easier for a toddler to handle egg-shaped crayons or oversized crayons, but using that standard size will help them build up the muscles they need to handle a pen or pencil appropriately.

The most notable writing tool from the Montessori method is salt writing or a salt tray. You can use the sandpaper letters, sandpaper numbers, or number and letter cutouts to help the child trace the shape with their finger. Then they make the same movement in the salt tray to write out the number or letter. You don't need a fancy tray or even fancy letter cutouts. You can do this activity on a budget, and if you haven't invested in sandpaper letters or numbers yet, you can simply write them out yourself and have your child trace over what you've written. The only thing to note here is that Himalayan salt or kosher salt does work better because the granules are not as fine, and they won't fall back into those holes as quickly. You can also use the same salt repeatedly. You are by no means wasting salt.

Finally, we will leave you with an activity that can grow with your child and helps the story building element of writing. Use either a chalkboard or dry erase board to encourage your child to explore writing independently. Most modern parents prefer dry erase boards to a chalkboard, but remember that chalkboards are harder to wipe away, and they may get a greater sense of reward from seeing their work remain in place rather than getting frustrated that the dry erases pen wipes away unintentionally.

They may not even use words for their writing. They may start storytelling with pictures. Don't worry because it is the same muscles holding that bit of chalk or that dry erase marker that they'll use to craft letters and numbers later in life. Storytelling is often neglected in traditional schools until they reach later grades. Instead, Kindergarten teachers and first-grade teachers often provide stories rather than engage the child in story building. By allowing your child to create a story through pictures or words on a chalkboard or a dry erase board, you develop two skills at once. Plus, storytelling is an engaging way to keep your child interested in writing and pursuing that interest.

Activities can help cultivate an interest in a numerical sense, reading, and writing. It is important to acknowledge that unlike traditional schools, Montessori children often learn to write and read when they're learning their alphabet and numbers. Instead of staggering the learning stage from learning the alphabet to the reading and writing alphabet, the learning process is ongoing. It may seem as though toddlers are taking longer to pick up on the alphabet or numbers if they're also learning to read and write them. However, you will reach a point where everything clicks into place.

Using all three activities at once, learning to read, write, and use number sense also allows your child to utilize their short attention span. This isn't something that most parents get to cash in on often, but toddlers have a short attention span. Don't try to sit your toddler down and teach them to write for 30-minutes straight. Instead, use fun activities to engage in writing, reading, and numerical learning. That way, they can jump from activity to activity, and they don't even realize that they're learning and developing the same skill.

Chapter 10: Interesting Arts and Crafts for Creative Toddler

By and large, the Montessori method engages children in a way that promotes creativity. Developing creativity at such a young age has drastically changed the lives of many who grew up with early Montessori education, even if they entered into traditional or standard education systems afterward. Creativity lends itself to our ability to think analytically and dive into problem-solving.

Without creativity, we cannot analyze data. We cannot construct or build structures. We could not solve the problems of the world. Although that seems like a scaling way out of proportion for toddlers, it comes down to just that. Creative kids become our strategic problem solvers. We've acknowledged in other chapters some all-stars from Montessori education, and among them is Will Wright. The creator of the Sims produced, built, and continues to generate something that the video game industry had not seen before. He offered a solution to the violent video game or story-driven video game culture. He presented a sandbox world for people to explore through an avatar of their own creation.

Now, where does creativity start? With the Montessori environment, there should be a variety of creative tools and outlets for the child. Toddlers are naturally creative, possibly because they don't have preconceived notions about how certain things should work. They don't pick up a crayon and think, "Oh, I need a piece of paper," they turn right to the wall and get busy. In this chapter, we look at specific arts and crafts that toddlers excel at, and we address the tools you need for these activities.

Arts and Crafts Build Imagination and More

Arts and crafts build imagination, creativity, self-confidence, boost self-exploration, but they also offer a lot of tangible or practical skills. While some parents encourage children to seek creative efforts for the sake of their imagination and creativity, others are more worried about real-world elements. Don't worry; if you're a parent who is more concerned about mathematics and science, you're not alone. But art and math aren't so different.

There are basic rules that come with art, and your child will learn those naturally. There are life skills that come with crafting. In fact, handicrafts play a role in systems such as the Girl Scouts and the Boy Scouts of America because they develop life skills and self-confidence.

Things to Keep in Mind

There are few things to remember when introducing Arts, crafts, and new activities involving creativity to your child. First, the material should always be accessible or at your toddler's height.

You might have some initial concern that your toddler has access to their crayons at all times without supervision, but there are ways to get around that concern. You can always choose washable or mess-free paint, crayons, and markers. And Crayola has a Color Wonder line that only works when the pens or paint contact special paper. This is excellent for parents that want the materials to be available all the time, but also don't want it all over the walls or floor.

The second thing to remember is the quality of the materials. Have you ever tried to color with half-melted crayons? While it isn't impossible and we should expect our children to develop resourcefulness, if you start with high-quality materials, they will last longer, and will be more enjoyable to work with. Toddlers are easily frustrated, and if they get frustrated every time they go to their crayon box or paint, they will just stop interacting with those items. Toddlers are masters of avoidance for managing frustration.

Finally, one of the most important elements to consider when putting together craft kits or material for a toddler is that less is more. One of the recurring lessons in the Montessori method is that we should not over-stimulate the children or provide too many options. You don't need a pocket watch with every color under the sun. Fewer supplies provide greater exploration because it relies on natural resourcefulness.

But wait, what about those great painters that have bottles and bottles and bottles of different colors? To give some context, the well-known painter Bob Ross works with only 13 colors. Every one of Ross's paintings relied on 13 foundational colors, and he mixed them as he painted. Toddlers don't need all 13 of those colors. It's a little comical to think I'm handing Alizarin Crimson to a two-year-old. You can actually start with just the primary colors. Red, yellow, and blue can easily mix to create a wide variety of painting options.

With crayons and markers, you might branch out into a 7 or 10 pack where they can have access to a wider variety but are still not overwhelmed with the options.

Don't discourage your child from using household items. If your toddler decides that a paper towel is better than copy paper or brown paper, then let it happen. Maybe the texture of the paper towels enticed them to try something new. It's these little moments of creative thinking that you don't want to put down.

Activities

So, what activities can your toddler do? Like most other sections of this book, thinking about your toddler's restrictions is slightly off the mark because the realm of creativity and crafting is almost endless. We have a collection of activities here that can get you started, but feel free to engage your own creativity and explore with your child how many arts and crafts options are really in your home. It's a fun way to connect with your kids.

Clip and Cut Activity

Depending on where you stand, the clip and cut activity could be one of the best or the worst parenting tips you've heard. In Montessori, children are given tools that are safe but do require supervision. The clip and cut activity is not something that you will leave your child alone with; this is a great activity for an observation period where you are sitting nearby and watching closely.

Hand your toddler a pair of kid-safe scissors and a stack of construction paper. They will figure out what to do quickly, although they do try to cut their hair. With your kid clipping away at construction paper, they're developing a pincer grip, but they're also creating shapes. If you start with a square piece or rectangular piece of construction paper, anything they cut out of that is a shape.

They are unknowingly creating triangles, circles, rectangles, rhombuses, and more. What happens with the clip and cut activity? Because it is largely self-led, they will find innate ways to pick up on these shapes. They don't have a name to give these shapes yet, and they don't realize there are proper ways to create a shape. They are taking raw activity and slowly refining it. For the clip and cut activity, the toddler will soon realize that some consistent shapes are arising from their activity, and then they will try to recreate those shapes again and again. Over just a few weeks, you might notice that your child went from slashing at the sides of the paper to cutting out a diamond shape carefully.

Unconventional Paintbrushes Activity

By the age of two or three, your child has probably had some experience with paintbrushes, and it can be fun to change the tool.

This is one creative activity that builds those problem-solving muscles in the brain. Imagine if you went to write a letter and had no pen or pencil? What would you do? That is what you're proposing to your child.

Similar to many other activities throughout this book, this activity is self-led. Prevent your child from using their paint, a piece of paper, or canvas, and instead of offering paintbrushes, provide pompoms, small squares of felt, twisted up pipe cleaners, and even crumpled plastic wrap. How long does it take before they experiment with the different results from each new painting tool? Do they have a favorite they seem to prefer? You can mix this up by swapping out paintbrushes about halfway through the activity. If your child seems to lose steam, offer a paintbrush and see if they prefer it over the alternative tools you've offered.

Mosaic Paper Punches Activity

If you have a handful of construction paper on hand, then you can grab a good old-fashioned hole punch and go to town. If you have specialized hole punches, you can provide larger circles or different shapes. In traditional schools, this lines up with a similar activity meant for middle schoolers where they use small hole punches to make many tiny circles and then use those to cover an existing picture.

In this activity, you will provide your toddler with the hole punch of remnants, the tiny little circles, and a blank piece of paper. Slightly sticky paper works excellently. However, you can also take a glue stick and liberally apply it to the paper so anything that falls on it will stick.

The toddlers can apply the hole punch remnants to the paper, stack them, throw them like confetti, it doesn't matter. Overtime, however, they'll see these small dots can come together to make a picture. Similar to Monet, you're encouraging your child to use an unexpected shape to create larger images.

If you're worried about the size of the hole punch remnants, you can fold over a piece of construction paper multiple times and then cut a single circle and have much larger circles for your toddler to use. With effort on the part of the adults, either way will probably result in a hand cramp. Some parents have turned to simply ordering stickers. Ordering circular stickers are not cheating, it just provides a sticky backing for basically the same size circle.

Play-Dough Activities

When talking about Montessori, we're rarely inclined to jump into corporate names such as Play-Doh. However, this activity boosts Sensorial development, creative play, and can even prolong their attention span because of how open-ended this activity is. Now you can make play-dough at home! Do not go out and buy Play-Doh; the Play-Doh you make at home might even last longer.

To make your own Play-Doh, mix two cups of flour, 3/4 cup of salt, four teaspoons of cream of tartar, two cups of Warm Water, two tablespoons of oil, and food coloring. You can mix all the ingredients except for the food coloring and then divide them into separate sandwich bags and color them that way.

Then hand the super soft and squishy play-dough to your kid on a cookie sheet. They can do whatever they want with this crafting material. They can wrap it around items. They can use stamps to stamp different shapes into place, or even use cookie cutters to cut out shapes.

Spaghetti Activities

There is a reason so many parents love doing crafts that involve spaghetti. First, it's cheap. Second, it's easy to put together; you just throw in some boiling water, and finally, it works so many muscles and skills. Wet spaghetti is difficult to hold on to, and it's slimy. By using cooked spaghetti for different crafts and activities, you can build up those fine muscles skills in your toddler's hands, boost their sensory exposure, and help them exercise their creativity.

What first? Your toddler can paint with spaghetti. Boil up some spaghetti and then put the spaghetti right into the paint. They can pick up a noodle and smear it across the paper or wax paper and create many designs that they probably couldn't achieve with paintbrushes. Alternatively, you can boil the spaghetti, coat it in margarine or butter, so it hardens up, and let it dry. Then, let your toddler lay out the cold noodles onto the paper, and paint over them with foam-tipped paintbrushes. Not only is this activity fun, but it is a lot less messy than you might expect from painting with pasta.

The next spaghetti activity can be used to make a wind chime, dreamcatcher, and really a wide variety of other shapes and figures as well. For example, while this started as an early activity for one little girl, Bella, with making a dreamcatcher, it turned into a winter activity and making snowflakes. Have your child dry spaghetti noodles and if they can handle it, a bit of glue, or play-dough that you don't mind drying out.

Then they can use the dry spaghetti noodles by snapping them into different lengths and sticking them with glue or play-dough to create a dreamcatcher, snowflakes, spider webs, and much more.

These activities are all meant to boost creativity, so do your best not to interject while the child is engaging in these activities. You might feel inclined to acknowledge that the paintbrush doesn't work that way, or the Play-Doh isn't meant for that. But honestly, there are so many uses available through arts and crafts materials that our toddlers may even teach us new and exciting ways to use the same old tools.

Chapter 11: Positive Discipline in the Montessori Home

Discipline is one of the most widely covered and controversial topics that appear in parenting books, on blogs, and in various other mediums. Social media is brimming with judgmental parents and non-parents who feel compelled to give their advice and insight. Try to bring in a judge-free mentality for this chapter because the Montessori discipline does spark a lot of controversies. Not only that, it preaches self-discipline, but it also preaches positive discipline and not encouraging your child.

Now, self-discipline is something we're all familiar with and is really something we expand on as adults. We learn the hard way we are responsible for our behavior, our reactions, and other elements of our life that until adulthood seem out of our control. Self-discipline, or the lack of it, is largely to blame for much of that teenage angst.

Diving into the positive discipline and the controversial element of encouraging your child or offering praise, it will take more than the brief touch on self-discipline. In this chapter, you'll find a variety of techniques largely regarded as positive discipline and have been found to build empathy and a cooperative relationship. The Montessori method is not the only system or belief pattern that offers positive discipline. Many pediatricians and child psychiatrists also support Maria Montessori's foundation for positive discipline. It's worth noting now; positive discipline sounds a little backward. Most of us were raised with good old traditional negative discipline, which is as bad as it sounds. Both parents not only believe that that's normal but don't know how else to approach discipline. It's not just spanking or going into a timeout. Negative discipline can also come in the form of how to talk to our children and how we behave when they don't act the way we want.

Through this chapter, we hope to give you the information, tools, and resources necessary for you to understand positive discipline and how to build self-discipline within your child.

We completely understand that every parent has a different approach to parenting. We hope that you'll consider promoting self-discipline and using the tools for positive discipline.

Be Proactive - The Foundation for Positive Discipline

One of the most highly commended personal development books is The 7 Habits of Highly Effective People. On its own, the book offers insight and advice beyond value for any adult, but, as a parent, it's worth coming back to that first habit of 'being proactive.' Being proactive establishes a level of fairness in the household when it comes to living with or engaging with a toddler. Toddlers may not know much about rules and may have little respect for authority in any capacity, but they understand fairness.

So how can you be proactive and build a foundation for positive discipline?

Make very clear rules that can't fall into any other interpretation. Toddlers and young children especially like to push boundaries, and if there's an opportunity to misinterpret a rule, they'll take it. So, make very clear, understandable, and consistent rules.

Examples of these can include:
- Only nice touching
- No biting people
- No hitting
- No slapping
- No kicking people or animals
- Clean up before starting a new activity

Ideally, these rules won't include the word "*no*" or "*don't,*" but there are only so many ways to phrase restriction on your toddler's freedom. Freedom with restrictions is the overarching concept within the Montessori method, and you're allowing your toddler a lot of freedom, but there are restrictions. Your toddler should not inflict physical harm on you or any other living creature. Your child will eventually have to learn to clean up and all variety of other life skills.

The trick to establishing a foundation has a few core rules; ones you can always revert back to, which is why rules such as "Only nice touching," work so well. When a child does something, you have to survey only whether that was nice touching or not nice touching (kicking, biting, and so forth).

The other way that you will work proactively to build a foundation of positive discipline is to cultivate a worry-free environment. You've already read the chapter on creating the Montessori environment, and we look at how eliminating likely dangers but promoting interest and engagement can help deter a lot of the times that parents have to tell their child to stop doing something. Essentially, eliminating the number of times you have to step into discipline will make your discipline efforts more effective. If your toddler is told "*no*" 50 times a day, any one of those times won't stand out more than the other 49 times they were told the word "*no.*" However, if you have to say "*no*" on a rare occasion, then it is impactful.

What is Self-Discipline?

The holy grail of most productive and happy adults is that they aren't overwhelmed and overstressed Type-A people. Self-discipline is the ability and the willingness of a person to monitor and correct their own behavior. This is something that we have to learn, and it's something that our children must learn. It's not a natural feature for most people. It is also often mis-attributed to willpower. Self-discipline and willpower are different things. You need not teach your child to abstain or persevere for the sake of willpower training.

So, how do you teach toddler self-discipline? Unfortunately, the best way to do it is to start removing or pulling back on things that we've enjoyed doing as parents: praise and reward. When children are told not to do something, and they face punishment, they only know not to do the thing because there's a punishment waiting. As with most things in life, the opposite is as true of this initial statement. When children are told to do something, and they know there's a reward, they only do it because of the reward.

Children and toddlers build self-discipline by learning the value of doing what's right and receiving the intrinsic reward of a job well done. Eventually, your child will take their dishes to the sink, not because you told them to and then thanked them afterward, but because they know that that is the right thing to do after they finish their plate. Eventually, your toddler will know to apologize after pushing down another kid unintentionally, because it's the right thing to do. Toddlers build self-discipline through these many small acts, acknowledging when they were at fault or acting without prompting from a reward or a punishment.

A note on discipline: parents all have different ways of disciplining, but there are differences between discipline and punishment. Punishing is what it sounds like, punishing a child for unwanted behavior. Whereas discipline is upholding established rules and standards. You'll use kindness and firmness to promote self-respect, self-discipline, cooperation, problem-solving, and desired behavior. Now, it is still frustrating. A screaming toddler is a screaming toddler, and sometimes mommy or daddy need a break.

But, over time, teaching or promoting self-discipline will make day-to-day life much easier.

How can you build self-discipline?

- Pull back on your praise - say thank you only when appropriate and give very specific compliments.

- E.g., Instead of, "*You're so smart*," use, "*You figured that out, can you show me how you did it?*"

- Show interest in your child's activities without telling them they're the best thing since sliced cheese - watch them, be present, and engage in the activity with them when invited. It means more than a passive compliment.

- Provide the opportunity to make meaningful choices.

- When faced with undesired behavior, try your best not to acknowledge it or excuse yourself.

- Have high expectations.

- Say "*yes*" more often than "*no*."

- Give simple and clear directions.

- Repeat expected rules often.

When put together, these small actions or mild changes and how you interact with your toddler can have a big impact on their self-discipline.

Elements of Positive Discipline

The key elements of positive discipline revolve around responsibility, cooperation, objective thinking, respect, courtesy, honesty, and compassion. Wouldn't we all love for our toddlers to understand and employ these elements often?

But a toddler's decision-making center of the brain simply isn't developed enough to acknowledge and act in line with these elements, all the time. The best you can do to put these positive elements into play in your household is to model those behaviors. Now, you might do that already, but your child doesn't know that. Your child doesn't have a name to give these actions, and they can't identify those actions in the moment. When do you notice there is a decision regarding responsibility, respect, honesty, or courtesy, point it out to your toddler. It can feel very self-absorbed at first, but by saying, "*I opened the door for someone because it was polite*," you're calling attention to that very specific action. Another example might be saying, "*Dad works with your sister during playtime, and that's why they have so much fun. They cooperate.*"

What Happens When Children Break the Rules?

Safety is always paramount, and sometimes, you can't talk your way through rule-breaking. This goes beyond the tantrums and bleeds into running into the street, or not holding hands in a parking lot. And there's another issue with getting out of their car seat. Those snazzy busy boards help kids learn how to open snaps and clips, making them car seat Houdinis.

When a child breaks the rules, there are a few ways to handle it. If safety is a factor, then removing them from the situation is often the best initial response. There is also the option of further restrictions on freedom. For example, if your child is constantly escaping their car seat, it may not be safe to take them out as often as you might have because they've shown there's a clear pattern they won't stay in their car seat when they need to for safety reasons. If they miss grocery trips, you might notice your toddler asking to go out with you, and then you can emphasize that they can go with you if they stay in their car seat. If they refuse to stay in their seat again, then you may choose not to take them out without help from another adult.

Biting, Scratching, Hair Pulling, and Other Physical Attacks

These issues are not as much of an emergency as they initially seem. It's developmentally appropriate. Your kid is not a bad kid, and the best approach is through proactive play. You can role-play with stuffed animals, where one stuffed animal gets hit, and the other animal says I don't like that and leaves. This is one of the few directed Montessori activities because it directly addresses how it is appropriate and respectful to touch or engage another person.

When it's directed toward you, stop their hands or feet, and say something like, "*I won't let you hit me.*" And emphasize that hitting/kicking hurt. One of the few times that Montessori aligns with outside teaching is in these moments. Positive parenting comes from a lesson seen in the Happiest Toddler on the Block and focuses on Kind Ignoring.

Kind ignoring is the act of removing yourself from the situation. Now, you don't want to shame or put down the child, but acknowledge that the behavior is not okay, it hurts, and you don't want it to happen to you. Acknowledge also that you will be back or available later.

- Try these:
- "*Mom doesn't like slaps. Mom will be back when you stop slapping.*"
- "*Dad doesn't like bites. They hurt. Dad wants alone time because these bites hurt.*"
- "*I don't like hits; they feel bad. I'll come back in a bit when you don't feel like hitting anymore.*"

These emphasize responsibility on their part and aren't a punishment, although your toddler won't feel that way. You have removed yourself from physical pain. That's not a punishment for your child, it's a relief for you. Now when you leave your child's area or room, just be sure that it's a safe place for them. If you've Montessori-styled your home, then you shouldn't have to worry about that.

Kind ignoring is also the go-to option for tantrums you can't talk through. In an ideal situation with positive discipline, you'll be able to sit down and discuss what happened when your child started their tantrum. Always intervene early before the tantrum gets out of hand.

You can acknowledge what they want or the things they can't find, but sometimes tantrums are just too emotional to reel in. Your toddler is an emotional being, and you have decades of logical thinking. The two don't align often. If you're getting frustrated, or you feel that you're tending toward negative discipline or physical punishment, kind ignoring can give you a break and a moment to decompress. Then you can get back into having that conversation with your toddler and de-escalate their fit.

Regarding Sharing

Montessori encourages more adult methods of sharing, which is complex because many Montessori teachers simply say they don't teach sharing. The model of sharing isn't that "everything is yours for the taking," which often adults jump in to present when they see children not sharing. Instead, Montessori emphasizes turn-taking. You are sharing the item, and that doesn't mean the child is forfeiting their time with the item simply because another child became interested in it. The second child can wait patiently until the first child has moved on.

Now, in public situations, sharing can get much more complex. You might encourage your child to learn specific words such as "turn," or "wait," to help them express they are not done with the toy yet. Particularly during toddler years, you'll have trouble because toddlers like to play next to each other but not necessarily with each other.

Whether you promote turn-taking over traditionally modeled toddler sharing where whoever had it first needs to give it up, or whoever had it first keeps the toy, is up to you.

Special Note for the Parents

Parenting is hard. Toddlers are prone to emotional outbursts, tantrums, and screaming fits for what seems like no reason. If committing to Montessori positive discipline sounds difficult, remember that you will still deal with tantrums, sharing problems, and outbursts no matter what discipline method you use. What it comes down to is which discipline method works best for you, and how that disciplined method impacts your relationship with the child.

With Montessori learning and encouragement, traditional discipline doesn't promote the level of independence that Montessori teaching does. Now your child is looking for a rule rather than looking at you to model your behavior. If a child encounters a new situation, they do what they want and suffer the consequences later. Whereas self-discipline and positive discipline help the child make more conscientious choices earlier.

Chapter 12: Growing Montessori

Toddlers don't just grow; they grow fast. You don't have to talk to an early childhood development specialist or psychiatrist to know that from day-to-day, week-to-week, and month-to-month, your toddler is quickly evolving into an different person. They do have core elements of their personality as a foundation. Still, they're learning at such a fast rate that not surprisingly, as adults we are so surprised at how quickly they move from one interest to another or from one challenge to another. Taking off shoes can be an impossible task one day, and easy-breezy the next.

So, one of the common questions that come up with Montessori in the home is how to accommodate such a fast-growing tiny person. Your toddler will inevitably grow and go through changes, both physically and mentally. You can apply the Montessori method to help acknowledge these changes. You can address topics such as clinginess, separation anxiety, tantrums, teething, potty training, and more.

We know that using the toddler Montessori discipline is only one step in your parental journey. We didn't want to leave you without all the information you might need to keep moving forward down this path with the Montessori method in mind. As you employ the

Montessori method with your toddler, a lot of the principles and foundational elements will become second nature. It can become easy to find times to observe, guide, and understand exactly how your child is trying to communicate. That gives you more license to advance in Montessori and guide your child through that process as you improve.

Key Times in Physical Development Happen in the Early Years

The key moments in physical development throughout the early years include teething, learning to pull themselves up, learning to crawl, learning to walk, learning to open and shut items, and more. Even at the toddler age, it may seem as though your child has hit the major physical development milestones. However, your toddler is still growing. Their perception is physically changing as they grow taller and build upon smaller physical development milestones.

The milestones many people overlook or simply don't know how to address during toddler years include developing the pincer grip, learning how to hold a crayon or pencil, operating scissors, and more fine-tuned movements.

Remember that most successful students have begun complex stringed instruments as young as three or four years old. Those instruments are demanding with finger movement and fine motor skills.

Toddlers are still developing their larger motor functions, most toddlers don't jump proficiently until about two and half years old, and many may have a slightly wonky run until they're about three or four.

While it is fun to have this information on hand, through Montessori guidance, it's also beneficial to know in terms of presenting activities. If you notice that your child can proficiently jump, then you can encourage more outdoor activity that require jumping or leaping. And if you notice that your child has no problem handling small objects with their hands, you might introduce a new instrument or new tools that require more delicate precision with handwork.

Growing Up Challenges

With the challenges of growing, especially at the rate that toddler's do, it's good to have a well-stocked tool belt for handling these issues. What is the Montessori method? We know that redirection is an powerful tool. Along with redirection, you can also encourage toddlers to play and you can provide engaging independent activities. The combination of these three can help address issues such as clinginess and separation anxiety.

If you have stopped by a Montessori School, you may have already seen this in action. Often when parents approach the new student, the Montessori teacher will take the child and guide them to nearby activities so the parent can leave after they've said goodbye. It drastically reduces the outbursts and creates a positive experience for the child. Now, when you're using Montessori at home, this may seem more of a challenge. You may need to take the initiative and have the other adult redirect attention so you can step away.

Clinginess and separation anxiety is an common challenge for toddlers. Most have spent more time with one parent than anyone else that they know. It can also seem as though that parent is leaving and will never come back.

Toddlers don't need a history of abandonment to have this worry that someone will not return. Some have not developed that understanding that things or people leave and come back. Saying goodbye peacefully and then redirecting your attention can be the key to reducing separation anxiety and clinginess. The Montessori method largely promotes the development of independence, especially from an early age.

As you promote that independence, the toddler may lapse into extreme clinginess. It is a common cause of backsliding. To help continue forward motion in building independence, you can establish "independent times" where you sit back and observe. During these times, you're not available for together play or providing help with challenges or struggles they can handle on their own. Independent time is actually a great opportunity for completely absent observation. Redirect their attention, let them know that you'll be back shortly, and then find a spot out of eyesight. If you notice your child needs help, use this as an opportunity to observe how they overcome the challenge.

For toilet training, potty training, or bathroom learning, this can be a particular challenge. You'll need a potty or seat for your toilet and then walk them through the potty process.

Toys that Grow with Them

Most of the Montessori tools are already meant to grow with your children. If they were in a Montessori School, you might notice that six and seven-year-olds are still playing with the Pink Tower and building blocks. With the modern age, most parents accept or believe that children tire of toys quickly and need new materials to remain engaged. While toddlers can become tired of seeing the same thing again and again, the idea with some of these toys is that you modify how you play with them. Then some toys may follow them even into teenage years and adulthood if the interest is developed and continued.

Let's tackle adjustable furniture first. What's the Montessori prepared environment, toddlers should have toddler size furniture. However, with adaptable cribs and toddler beds, you can invest in one piece of furniture that can grow with your child. The same is possible with moving from a highchair to a booster seat, to removing the seat all together for sitting at the table. A toddler seat or couch may simply enter retirement after the child has outgrown it. Some furniture type materials such as art easels are usually adjustable.

When looking at musical tools, you might have to pay special attention to instruments that don't require scaling. We're not talking about musical scales. We're talking about size. You simply cannot purchase an adult violin and expect a four-year-old to handle it well. You would need a smaller, or to-scale, violin.

However, we don't scale down pianos or drums. There are "kid" versions of these, which use cheaper materials and aren't built to last. But a four-year-old can learn piano on a full-size piano. A child can learn to drum on full-size drum sets. If you are looking to invest in instruments, then you might prioritize instruments that won't need full replacement every other year.

Water play can also grow with your child. While they may show a special interest in plungers, pictures, and even water wheels for pouring in their early years, they may enjoy more advanced activities as we approach the ages of five or six. Allowing them to construct waterways or direct water traffic can be an exciting way to change a water pouring station. Water is enjoyable at almost any age, and it comes with unmatched benefits in terms of learning the water cycle and the basics of physics. Our world largely functions on water, and keeping that interest peaked at a young age can help them understand its role in our world later in life.

Blocks and stacking blocks are another big-ticket item that can grow with your child. Even at the ages of 11 or 12, blocks can be a part of everyday play. Your toddler may have simply stacked up a tower and then knocked it over. Now, older children might build castles, create bridges, or even create designs and shapes that are unique but recognizable.

One of the common questions that parents of growing children ask about Montessori involves play. The question is usually, is doll play considered Montessori learning? Now, dolls and dollhouses rarely have a place in Montessori schools. Because of the importance and focus given to the scientific method, these creative or open-ended play are often left to the home environment. There is nothing that would allude to Maria Montessori being against doll play. In fact, many children use dolls for reenacting everyday situations and use them to explore conversation and interaction. All of those elements are present in the majority of Montessori activities. It seems a little ridiculous, but generally, you would aim toward a less guided play environment. What we're getting down to is that dolls, dollhouses, cars, and furniture are just fine. They're actually great because of how long children will play with dolls throughout their childhood and even into early adolescence. However, you might choose a doll with a house rather than a doll and a doctor's coat with a doctor's office. Allow your child to recreate those things using materials they have at home, let them bring creativity to doll play rather than relying on preconceived environments.

Parenting Habits Change and Adapt

As a toddler goes through tantrums and potty training, two of the most common challenges for parents, you can change and adapt your habits to promote development. Many parents cite that potty training is one of the keystones in developing conversations. You not only have to address the function of the toilet and the necessity of potty training, but also addressing concerns and fears that the toddler has associated with potty training.

Have Conversations

The famous book entitled The Montessori Toddler, from Simone Davis, covered a specific challenge in allowing your toddler to have a tantrum. It encouraged parents to acknowledge the child's feelings and walk them through processing those feelings. Not every parent is prepared to do this in every environment that toddlers have tantrums. In fact, most publications that cover this particular element from this book don't cite the most problematic times that toddlers have tantrums. However, there's a bit of a twist. When you use this method ahead of time, it becomes a proactive way of developing conversations that are effective and fast. When a growing toddler or child is having a tantrum at home, you can take your time to walk them through exactly what's happening. But also do this when they're not having tantrums. After your toddler becomes a child, they are taking one more step toward adulthood, and what they need from you is a conversation. They don't need a pandering voice saying, "*Oh, I understand that you are sad.*" They need someone who's going to talk to them like a person.

When your toddler has that tantrum, or has to face that fear of the potty, or is having trouble sleeping on their own after so many years of the family bed, that is the time to have the hard conversations. Then, when your toddler goes into tantrum mode in a grocery store, you can have that fast and efficient conversation to wrap it up quickly and get on with your shopping.

There is a hard to identify moment in development where children go from needing you to mimic what's happening, to you setting the tone for the conversation that's happening. Earlier in this book, we cited mimicking tantrums and repeating what your toddler was saying. Now, when your child can communicate what they want, or it's clear that they feel the situation is unjust or targeted against them, you can engage in a different type of conversation. You can start with that original mimicking. You can say something like, "Reina, you are so mad that he has candy, and I'm not letting you have any." with the statement, you are acknowledging their feelings and site the core of the tantrum. They saw another kid with candy, they asked you for candy, you told them no, end of the story. Now, for the sake of consistency and maintaining a respectful relationship between your decision-making and their existence in the world, you can't give in to their demands for candy every time. You can, however, have a conversation.

Patience Stretching

With tantrums, listening skills, and continuing development through childhood years, your kid needs some patience. Patience is a vital life skill, but it also helps to deter tantrums and increase listening skills. Patience stretching is one of the guided elements of Montessori, and it spreads to many other methods of positive discipline.

When your kid has a tantrum, or even a toddler starts to throw a tantrum, get them to scale it down by counting. This is mildly redirecting their attention. You aren't setting them on a completely different course; you are putting the tantrum on pause. You can count to three, five, or even ten, and when you see that their breathing has started to calm down, you can begin the patience stretching.

To exercise patience stretching, get the toddler to count to 10 calmly. You can start first, take a deep breath and say "*one*," and wait for them to repeat. Then when you get to 10, you can say, "*Okay, now ask me nicely.*" Usually, this works, but do this when there aren't tantrums happening.

You can build this skill by using patient stretching and everyday activities. If your child is stacking blocks, then ask them to count with you before stacking the next block. You can also do this when you're getting ready to sit down and eat. Patience stretching is not a reward. There will be plenty of times you will need to rely on patience stretching just to calm down a tantrum, and even then, the child may not get their way.

As your child grows, you'll see the benefits of patient stretching, having conversations, and having tools that grow with your child. Not only will it foster greater independence, but you'll can see them adapt to their changing environment. The Montessori method is not just for early childhood development; it can follow them well into their teenage years and even adulthood.

Conclusion

Thank you for reading, and we hope that you've found all the resources necessary to get started with Montessori learning for your child. Toddlers are a challenge, but with the Montessori method, you can spend time watching them with a new fascination for how their tiny minds work and develop. Use the Montessori discipline for toddlers to help build up the creative thinking, language, mathematics, coordination, and problem-solving abilities of your child.

Through these activities, you can support creativity and engage their minds in new and unexpected ways. Get them up and moving with music and movement, or have their little fingers hard at work, sorting out differently colored objects. These activities are fun for toddlers, and, usually, they're pretty easy for the adults to set up and monitor.

Start by creating the right environment for Montessori engagement by thoughtfully placing toys and other objects. Then move on to presenting activities that are age appropriate but still present a challenge. Finally, keep growing by encouraging further sensory and coordination development along with those smarts your child is already showing!

Here's another book by Meryl Kaufman that you might like

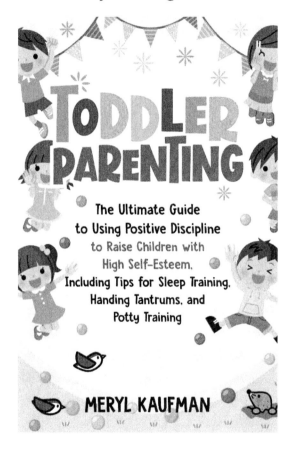

References

https://www.youtube.com/watch?v=gRZD0Y01xmI

https://www.italiansrus.com/articles/whoami6.htm

https://amshq.org/About-Montessori/History-of-Montessori/Who-Was-Maria-Montessori

https://www.livingmontessori.com/montessori-method/history-of-the-montessori-method/

https://www.montessori.edu/FAQ.html

https://www.public-montessori.org/montessori/.

https://www.montessorieducation.com/blog/alexander-graham-bell-and-montessori

https://www.bartleby.com/essay/Describe-in-Detail-the-Three-Elements-of-FKDK6CS5H3U4Z1.

https://amshq.org/About-Montessori/What-Is-Montessori/Terminology

https://www.retrogamer.net/retro_games90/the-making-of-the-sims/

https://www.newamerica.org/weekly/bezos-montessori-education/

https://www.montessorieducation.com/blog/jeff-bezos-amazon-just-gave-1-billion-to-montessori-inspired-preschools-now-what-is-montessori

https://www.edweek.org/ew/articles/2018/09/26/the-montessori-mafia-why-tech-titans-like.html https://indianamontessoriacademy.org/eight-principles-of-montessori-education/https://indianamontessoriacademy.org/eight-principles-of-montessori-education/

https://montessori-nw.org/about-montessori-education

http://psychosocialdisney.blogspot.com/2015/07/well-begun-is-half-done.html

https://www.youtube.com/watch?v=GhANk9tIW9s

https://montessoriacademy.com.au/montessori-education/montessori-principles-education/

http://forestmontessori.com/brain-development-from-birth-to-three-years/

https://www.kidcentraltn.com/development/1-3-years/brain-development-toddlers-1-3-years.html

http://images.pcmac.org/SiSFiles/Schools/CA/SMJUHSD/PioneerValleyHigh/Uploads/DocumentsSubCategories/Documents/Chapter08_WHYL-A.pdf

https://nancyguberti.com/5-stages-of-human-brain-development/

https://www.youtube.com/watch?v=XmMhQD84_1E

https://theeducatorsroom.com/being-a-parent-and-a-teacher-an-impossible-combination/

https://www.psychologicalscience.org/observer/perception-and-play-how-children-view-the-world

https://www.youtube.com/watch?v=DZUhxuKyucM

https://www.youtube.com/watch?v=ypR-P1gAfas

https://www.montessoriprintshop.com/observation.html

https://www.youtube.com/watch?v=xVHJlIch5nk

https://www.youtube.com/watch?v=YaCbwVARh5I

https://www.youtube.com/watch?v=pp7iH4qhPtM

https://www.montessoriteachered.com/the-montessori-muse-blog/2018/8/15/a-montessori-manor-how-to-help-parents-incorporate-a-montessori-mindset-at-home

https://www.healthlinkbc.ca/health-topics/ue5465

https://www.goodstart.org.au/news-and-advice/october-2016/exploring-the-benefits-of-sensory-play

https://www.youtube.com/watch?v=_wq3jpl7GUc

https://www.youtube.com/watch?v=PC6vKh3bhTI

https://www.themontessorinotebook.com/age-appropriate-chores-for-children/

https://www.mother.ly/child/montessori-ways-your-toddler-can-help-around-the-house

https://www.youtube.com/watch?v=WT5ViWO24xk

https://voilamontessori.com/montessori-children-and-chores/

https://www.youtube.com/watch?v=4Uyzls0Xs0U

https://www.azquotes.com/quote/1206104

https://nycaieroundtable.org/2019/03/13/what-are-the-benefits-of-music-for-babies-and-toddlers/

https://nafme.org/music-education-montessori-lens-every-child-musical-potential/

https://www.montessoriservices.com/ideas-insights/music-in-the-montessori-classroo

https://www.montessoriservices.com/music-movement/instruments

https://www.themontessorinotebook.com/montessori-and-music/

https://livingmontessorinow.com/montessori-inspired-music-activities-for-toddlers-and-preschoolers/

http://www.montessori-blog.org/2018/05/16/famous-people-who-attended-montessori-beyonce-knowles/

https://www.youtube.com/watch?v=YvybLbW_D5Q

https://momtessorilife.com/2015/09/04/language-photo-cards-family/

https://www.youtube.com/watch?v=vmqen3cueuY

https://livingmontessorinow.com/learning-to-read-can-be-just-a-fun-game/

https://guidepostmontessori.com/blog/teaching-reading-writing-montessori

https://www.youtube.com/watch?v=Qq90WOn3xAY

https://www.everystarisdifferent.com/2016/01/learning-montessori-way-writing.html

https://blog.workman.com/2019/04/montessori-method-encourage-creativity-child/

https://thomaspark.co/2015/11/bob-ross-color-palette-in-css/

https://www.howwemontessori.com/how-we-montessori/crafts/

https://mymodernmet.com/pointillism-art-georges-seurat/

https://www.iheartnaptime.net/play-dough-recipe/

https://www.instructables.com/id/How-to-use-spaghetti-to-paint-like-Jackson-Pollock/

https://blog.hubspot.com/sales/self-discipline

http://ageofmontessori.org/teach-children-self-discipline-instead-obedience/

https://www.youtube.com/watch?v=SckUevGH-Pk

https://www.livingmontessori.com/positive-discipline-and-child-guidance/

https://www.youtube.com/watch?v=nt9ck98l8Uo

https://www.howwemontessori.com/how-we-montessori/2011/08/my-baby-is-teething.html

https://www.montessoridowntown.com/handle-a-clingy-toddler/

https://www.youtube.com/watch?v=iL_vvFAH8AY

https://www.themontessorinotebook.com/stop-tantrum-yes-read-right/

https://www.familyeducation.com/life/communicating-your-toddler/how-have-conversation-your-three-year-old

https://www.happiestbaby.com/blogs/toddler/teaching-patience-toddlers

Printed in Great Britain
by Amazon